"More than anything else the success of soft drinks depends on taste and **positioning**, rather than on presentation and design."

Food Magazine (Holland)

"Novell is **positioning** its next generation of Unix System V as an inexpensive yet scalable platform that helps NetWare users."

Communications Week

"Rolls-Royce to buy Allison, **positioning** U.K. firm in the U.S."
The Wall Street Journal, Europe Edition

"Our **positioning** strategy of our dog food is critical to our profit."

MANAGING DIRECTOR
Pet Food Company (Australia)

"As Intel Corp. adjusts course in the wake of its Pentium problems, rival chipmakers are **positioning** themselves to benefit from the potential competitive opportunity."
Business Marketing

"Analysts believe that Granada is **positioning** itself to make a full bid if the prohibitive takeover rules are relaxed."
The Times of London

"Sun Microsystems has begun **positioning** itself as a killer of mainframes, and is pumping up sales of servers, midrange computers that link personal computers and workstations."
The Wall Street Journal

"**Positioning** Genzyme as a health care company represents lower risk for the investor and the company."
Boston Globe

"For those who thought that Mercedes' target audience consisted solely of blue-haired CEOs, times have changed. With repricing and **repositioning**, Germany's luxury leader is on the offensive."

Brandweek

W9-AUZ-400

The New
Positioning

Other Books by Jack Trout

Coauthored with Al Ries

The New Positioning

The Latest on the World's #1 Business Strategy

Jack Trout
with Steve Rivkin

McGraw-Hill, Inc.
New York   San Francisco   Washington, D.C.   Auckland   Bogotá
Caracas   Lisbon   London   Madrid   Mexico City   Milan
Montreal   New Delhi   San Juan   Singapore
Sydney   Tokyo   Toronto

Library of Congress Cataloging-in-Publication Data

Trout, Jack.
    The new positioning : the latest on the world's #1 business
strategy / Jack Trout with Steve Rivkin.
        p.   cm.
    Updated ed. of: Positioning / Al Ries. lst ed., rev. c1986.
    Includes index.
    ISBN 0-07-065291-0
    1. Positioning (Advertising)   I. Rivkin, Steve.   II. Ries,
Al. Positioning.   III. Title.
    HF5827.2.R53   1995
    659.1'11—dc20   95-22196
                                                           CIP

    2 3 4 5 6 7 8 9 0   BKP/BKP   9 0 0 9 8 7 6 5

ISBN 0-07-065291-0

*The sponsoring editor for this book was Philip Ruppel, the editing
supervisor was Jane Palmieri, and the production supervisor was
Donald Schmidt. It was set in Fairfield by Victoria Khavkina of
McGraw-Hill's Professional Book Group composition unit.*

Printed and bound by Quebecor/Book Press.

McGraw-Hill books are available at special quantity discounts to
use as premiums and sales promotions, or for use in corporate
training programs. For more information, please write to the
Director of Special Sales, McGraw-Hill, Inc., 11 West 19th Street,
New York, NY 10011. Or contact your local bookstore.

 This book is printed on recycled, acid-free paper con-
taining a minimum of 50% recycled, de-inked fiber.

To Al Ries,
my longtime partner in positioning

Contents

Introduction

Many in the world think positioning is a relatively new idea. The reason: Unlike concepts such as "excellence," "quality," or "reengineering," which exploded on the scene, "positioning" snuck up on the business world.

The first words on the subject go back 25 years, when I wrote an article in *Industrial Marketing* magazine entitled "Positioning is a game people play in today's me-too marketplace."

The earth didn't tremble, and the event went unnoticed.

This was followed by more articles and many speeches, and 15 years ago Al Ries and I wrote the book *Positioning: The Battle for Your Mind.*

Because "positioning" ended up leaking into the business scene, it still seems like a fresh, new concept. Which is why it was mentioned 16,917 times in U.S. publications last year.

Well, as the one who started it all, I can safely say that the concept needs updating.

New Information on the Mind

We've* always defined "positioning" not as what you do to the product, but what you do to the *mind*.

The ultimate marketing battleground is the mind, and the better you understand how the mind works, the better you'll

---

*You'll notice in certain sections, especially the case histories, that I use the editorial "we." That's because I'm describing work done with my longtime associate Al Ries, or other partners here and around the world.

understand how positioning works.

This is why we've continued to study the mind and how it takes in, stores, or rejects information. Part 1 of this book will present much of this new information. We'll even wheel in a number of psychologists to offer their views.

Change has become an ever-increasing factor in today's high-speed world. It's also something I never dealt with in my early work on positioning.

But as the years rolled by, I began to run into two basic types of companies with problems.

The first type had lost their focus in the mind of the marketplace. And they had done it to themselves, through things like line extension or diversification. An example would be Chevrolet. Once upon a time, this was America's family car. Good solid value. Today a Chevrolet is a big, small, cheap, expensive sports car, sedan, and truck. Chevrolet is no longer "the heartbeat of America." Ford is the number-one brand. Chevy needs to get back to basics.

The other type of change-related problem I noticed was the market changing underneath a company. To survive, they had to find a new idea or positioning to carry them forward. Lotus Development was an example of this, as their spreadsheet business became a mature business under attack from the high-tech Godzilla called Microsoft. (I discuss this at greater length in Chapter 8.)

"Repositioning" is the answer to these types of marketing problems. That's why this book will spend a great deal of time focusing on "repositioning," and how you go about it. It can be a very tricky piece of work. Case studies will play an important part in Part 2.

Much More Has Been Learned

Finally, practice makes perfect. Or if not perfect, at least a lot better.

In the 25 years since "positioning" first made its debut, I've worked with my partners on hundreds of positioning projects—from caskets to computers, and just about everything in between.

This work has taken me all over the world. En route, I've learned some tricks of the trade that weren't shared in the earlier writings. Part 3 will present some of them, like the power of sound, the latest on names, the problems of research, and simply telling it like it is as opposed to being cute about it. That section alone just may be worth the price of the book.

So read on. *The New Positioning* contains the final word on "positioning." If you don't get it this time, you're on your own.

Jack Trout

The New Positioning

PART ONE

Understanding the Mind

The brain has remained a mystery because it is so hard to access. The 1.4 kilos of soft pink and gray tissue is wrapped in a tough skin, padded by a bath of cerebral spinal fluid, and encased in a bone-hard shell. Except for an elite crew of neurosurgeons and scientists, no one has ever witnessed a brain at work. Most conclusions about brain function have been drawn from the study of people whose brains have been damaged by stroke, injury, or congenital defects.

BARBARA BUELL
Charting Brain Functions

Minds Can't Cope

W hile the mind may be a mystery, we know one thing for certain: it's under attack.

In *Positioning: The Battle for Your Mind*, we made a great deal of the fact that America has become the world's first "overcommunicated" society. The explosion of media forms and the ensuing increase in the volume of communications have dramatically affected the way people either take in or ignore the information offered them. Overcommunication has changed the whole game of communicating with and influencing people.

Well, what I thought was "overload" in the '70s turns out to be just warming up In the '90s. Here are some statistics that dramatize the problem:

- More information has been produced in the last 30 years than in the previous 5000 years.

- The total of all printed knowledge doubles every four or five years.

- One weekday edition of *The New York Times* contains more information than the average person was likely to come across in a lifetime in seventeenth-century England.

- More than 4000 books are published around the world every day.

- The average white-collar office worker uses 250 pounds of copy paper a year. That's twice the amount consumed 10 years ago.

Now, as you probably noticed, all those statistics deal with the printed form of communication. What about the electronic side of our overcommunicated society?

Electronic Overcommunications

Everywhere you travel in the world, satellites are beaming endless messages into every corner of the globe. By the time a child in the United Kingdom is 18, he or she has been exposed to 140,000 TV commercials. In Sweden, the average consumer receives 3000 commercial messages a day.

In terms of advertising messages, 11 countries in Europe broadcast well over 3 million television commercials in 1992.

Meanwhile, back in the United States, the electronic side of overcommunications is just warming up. Experts tell us we'll be going from 50 channels of television to 500. Can you imagine clicking through that many channels? By the time you find something you want to watch, you'll be just in time for the closing credits!

Suffering from a side effect of all this are the famous French bistros, which according to *The New York Times* are dying in droves. As one bistro owner lamented: "The Parisians are becoming like Americans. They're in a hurry. They buy takeout food instead of sitting down and eating in peace. At night they rush off to watch television."

And then there's all those computers, and the much-hyped information superhighway, which promises to deliver massive amounts of information to your home via fiber-optic cables, or CD-Roms, or whatever. (In 1975, there were only 300 on-line databases available. Now you can engulf yourself in 7900 databases with literally billions of bits of information.) If it all comes true, a number of people will have to be treated for *encyclophobia*—the fear of being trapped in an electronic encyclopedia.

Are People Getting Smarter?

As volume increases, is any of this information getting into people's brains?

In terms of language, there doesn't appear to be much progress. For example, the English language now contains roughly half a million usable words, five times more than during the time of Shakespeare. Even so, the average American recognizes only about 20,000 of them. The vocabulary of television news reports is limited to 7000 words.

In terms of retaining information, a German pioneer in scientific memory research has found that within 24 hours, people forget up to 80 percent of what they thought they had learned. (Every student has had that experience when cramming for tests.)

In terms of information availability, some scientists are so inundated with technical data that they claim it takes less time to conduct an experiment than to find out whether that experiment has been done before.

Now, let's say you really want to get smart, stop watching football, and start to read up on all that information. For example's sake, let's go back to *The New York Times*. One fat Sunday edition of *The New York Times* had more than 1600 pages, weighed 12 pounds, and contained more than 10 million words.

Reading 18 hours a day, at a fast reading speed of 500 words per minute, it would take you *18 days* to read everything in that one newspaper! By then, of course, you'd have two weeks' worth of unread newspapers piled up.

It's no wonder someone has said, "We're publishing more and reading less."

What About Smart Television Sets?

Perhaps you're thinking that reading a big newspaper would be silly. You'd rather do it all electronically, which should be quicker and more efficient. Well, much has been written about how the home television set will become more like a computer (and vice versa). People will sit in front of this wondrous machine and watch shows, read news, play games, interact, compute, shop, you name it.

I doubt that all of this will happen, but what if it did? Will these marvelous machines really make people smarter? Will they think better? The answer may lie with the folks who have had access to information-loaded computers for years. Are *they* getting smarter?

Are Computers Bad for Your Mind?

One of America's best thinkers, Edward de Bono, author of 40 books on creative thinking, recently declared in an article that "thinking in America is a lost art." And what passes for thinking is "seriously flawed."

His take is that multiple causes of problems tend to paralyze people, to the point of *analyzing* more and more and *thinking* less and less. When one looks at the problems besetting many of our best and brightest companies today, one would say that his thesis is correct. And yet these companies have invested millions in computers and networks, to enhance the thinking ability of their managers.

Consider the Digital Equipment Corporation, a company in some difficulty. Digital was one of the earlier pioneers in the use of E-mail. When you strolled through their offices in the early '80s you couldn't help but be impressed by the acres of desktop machines, all wired together and spitting out information and messages from around the world.

One day I was in the office of Stan Olsen, brother of ex-CEO Ken Olsen and one of DEC's founders. I asked him how he liked electronic mail. His reply surprised me: "Let me tell you about E-mail. A lot of people send me messages. At the end of the day, when I print out my messages, I get a 30-foot roll of paper. There's no way I'll read all that. The way to get me is on the phone."

The problem is still with us. A 1994 survey of executive secretaries indicated that over 50 percent said they have no rational policy on E-mail use.

The More Information, the More Confusion

As problems have grown at Digital as well as other large, highly computerized companies like GM, IBM, and Sears, their stories point to the problems of too much information.

It's becoming apparent that a multibillion-dollar computer investment hasn't helped these companies to think very clearly. Quite to the contrary. I'm beginning to suspect that the more information these computers spit out, the more people get confused by it.

The problem is a disease called *clutter*. We are strangling ourselves with a cord of unnecessary words, too many statistics, and meaningless jargon. Solving a problem requires that we strip away all of the extraneous information and get to the heart of it. Jack Welch, General Electric chairman and CEO, put it all in perspective when he was interviewed by the *Harvard Business Review*:

> Insecure managers create complexity. Frightened, nervous managers use thick, convoluted planning books and busy slides filled with everything they've known since childhood. Real leaders don't need clutter. People must have the self-confidence to be clear, precise, to be sure that every person in their organization—highest to lowest—understands what the business is trying to achieve. But it's not easy. You can't believe how hard it is for people to be simple, how much they fear being simple. They worry that if they're simple, people will think they're simple-minded. In reality, of course, it's just the reverse. Clear, tough-minded people are the most simple.

Things Are Getting Worse

The problems I first began to talk about many years ago are only getting worse, as technology generates more and more information for minds that just can't keep pace.

If anything, I suspect that people are blocking out more and more information, as a self-defense mechanism against the rising tide of information.

All this means that whether your business efforts succeed or fail will depend on how well you have understood five statements about the most important mental elements in the positioning process:

1. Minds are limited.
2. Minds hate confusion.
3. Minds are insecure.
4. Minds don't change.
5. Minds can lose focus.

Minds Are Limited

Marketing people and people's minds are often in conflict.

Marketing people love to sit down and create carefully crafted arguments on behalf of their products. They are beautiful rationales to behold. Ripe with reasons, benefits, and facts.

Unfortunately, these arguments are being presented to minds that really aren't up to dealing with all that glorious information.

Our perceptions are selective. And our memory is *highly* selective.

We are cursed with the physiological limitation of not being able to process an infinite amount of stimuli.

Seeing is not akin to photographing the world, merely registering an image. Memory is not a tape recorder that stores information when we turn it on.

The First Hurdles

First, your message has to get by the mind's "volume control."

If one thinks of the human brain as a complex biological computer, then the synapse—the point at which a nerve impulse is transmitted—functions as a volume control. This is a powerful concept, because if it weren't for the buffer provided by the synapses, a single notion injected into one neuron in the brain's dense web would spread like wildfire in every direction—resulting in a massive cerebral short circuit.

Once you've passed this buffer, you're into short-term memory. Unfortunately, you're also in for short shrift. Short-term memory is very limited as to the amount of information it can hold, and the length of time it can hold it without reinforcement.

Fifty years ago, Harvard psychologist George Miller proposed that only seven "chunks" of information, like seven brands in a category, can easily be held in short-term memory.

Indeed, for most people, seven items—such as the seven digits of a phone number—can be held only for a few seconds, perhaps a minute, if they're not repeated. We call this The Rule of Seven. The number *eight* brand is out of luck.

We'll prove it with a pop quiz for all you frequent travelers. The top seven rental-car companies in America are Hertz, Avis, Alamo, Budget, National, Dollar, and Thrifty. Now: Who's number eight? (Answer: Who cares!)

Seven is enough for any traveler to remember. So the fleets vying to be number eight—it would be Value, Payless, or Advantage—are flat out of luck.

When something is placed in short-term memory, it will soon be lost forever unless something happens to transfer it over to long-term memory. Some psychologists estimate that 80 percent of short-term memory never does get transferred.

Also, short-term memory appears to be more auditory than visual, whereas long-term memory can be both. "Even when you read, to hold what you read in short-term memory, you translate it, you record it as it sounds," says Nobel laureate Herbert Simon, who has studied memory. Thus, short-term memory seems to operate better when something is spoken rather than written. (For more on this very important point, see Chapter 14, "Minds Work by Ear.")

The next issue we must deal with is the nature of what's being presented to the mind.

Information versus Data

In a landmark 1949 treatise entitled *The Mathematical Theory of Communications,* the authors defined information as "that which reduces uncertainty." If so, then the great "Information Age" is really an explosion of *non*-information. It is an explosion of *data*. What the Internet hucksters won't tell you is that the Internet is an ocean of unedited data, without any pretense of completeness. Lacking editors, reviewers, or critics, the Internet has become a wasteland of unfiltered data.

What's the difference between *data* and *information?*

Information must lead to *understanding*. Therefore, what constitutes information to one person may be mere data to another.

If it doesn't make sense to you, it's not information.

Consumers couldn't be convinced that Grapefruit Tang would have the taste of a superior grapefruit drink, because of the strong taste and content associations of the Tang orange drink.

Campbell Soup dubbed their line of spaghetti sauces Prego, after they found that the Campbell name left a connotation of a sauce that was orange and watery.

The Gallo jug-wine name will never wow the crystal-goblet set. The tony Four Seasons restaurant in New York offered a bottle of Gallo's Cabernet Sauvignon. The restaurant's manager called the wine "excellent," but said they sold only one bottle a week. "When people come to The Four Seasons, they don't dare to order a wine with such a name."

Rings of Defense

In an overcommunicated environment, people are selective as to the information they will accept. They get very defensive about what's being presented to them. It's a self-defense mechanism against sheer volume.

Social scientists say that our selectivity process has at least three rings of defense.

Selective *exposure* is the outermost ring. (I refuse to go to the opera. I won't watch that show or read that magazine.)

Then comes selective *attention*. (Good, my new issue of *The Wine Spectator* has arrived.)

Finally, there's selective *retention*. (I think I'll try that Pinot Noir from Oregon next time.)

People can head off unwanted or undesirable information by not exposing themselves to it, not paying attention to it, or not retaining it.

We tend to perceive the things that relate to our preexisting interests and attitudes—either to support them or to refute them.

People also have a tendency to misperceive and misinterpret communications according to those beliefs. Thus, every listener tends to hear his or her own message.

Interest and Memory

How much of your message gets through depends to a large part on what you're selling, according to years of data compiled by the Starch organization on readership scores by advertising category.

For instance, an advertisement for footwear is going to be twice as interesting as an ad for floor coverings, regardless of the brand names or benefits.

Similarly, an ad for perfume—most any perfume—is going to have double the average readership of a furniture ad.

A domestic car ad will be absorbed by only two-thirds as many readers as an ad for an imported car.

We've even discovered what I would call a "no-interest" category. That's right, a category where people will remember *no* brand names. It's *caskets*. Even when I tell you the leading brand name (Batesville), you will have forgotten it three paragraphs from now.

That's just the way it is. These interest levels, these biases, are firmly in place before we even pick up a magazine or newspaper.

In many ways, learning is simply remembering what we're interested in. Leonardo da Vinci put it very well when he said: "Just as eating against one's will is injurious to health, so study without a liking for it spoils the memory, and it retains nothing it takes in."

Emotions and Memory

The emotions play a big role in memory. "Simply stated, material learned when one is happy is better recalled when one is happy, and material learned when one is sad is better recalled when one is sad," according to an article in the *American Journal of Psychiatry.*

This phenomenon occurs because memory is tied closely to the limbic system, the brain's seat of emotions.

Parts of the limbic system act as selector switches to decide whether information should be recorded in the brain, according to research from the National Institute of Mental Health.

You can see or hear something once, and it can last not just minutes but a lifetime. There are times when memories are so intertwined with emotions that information is stored that we never intended to store. The most familiar example is John F. Kennedy's assassination.

If you're over the age of 45, you know where you were the moment you heard he was shot. Is that important? What difference does it make, *where* you were when you heard that news? Yet *that's* what we remember. That's what is stored.

When the emotional context is right, certain transmitters are turned on and a very solid message print is recorded in the brain. In the case of shocking or traumatic experiences, many more of the circumstances surrounding the information get recorded.

The Michelin Babies

Tires represent an example of a low-interest category. Buying a car is fun. Buying tires is a drag. Thank goodness we don't have to buy them very often.

This natural lack of interest explains why advertising tires is a difficult problem. The minute a tire ad appears on your TV screen, your mind immediately goes into a defensive mode.

Michelin has found a very successful way to get around these defenses. They use one of the most powerful emotional symbols in the business as a way of encouraging memory.

They use little babies sitting in tires.

These little tykes not only keep people watching and remembering but they communicate "safety," one of the most important attributes of a tire. (This tire will keep your little ones safe.)

But emotion has to be used carefully in advertising. It must be used only as a way to communicate a selling idea or benefit.

Lots of emotion and very little selling is one way to get people to like your commercial. But it won't get them to buy your product, as they will remember no reason to buy it.

Past Experience and Memory

Friedrich Nietzsche once wrote that "A man has no ears for that to which experience has given him no access."

In other words, we learn something new, only relative to something we already understand.

This is comparative learning, making connections between one piece of information and another.

Among learning theorists it is known as *apperception*, a concept first advanced in the nineteenth century.

Apperception may be defined as *the process of understanding by which newly observed qualities are related to past experience.*

In other words, when new ideas associate themselves with old ones.

Psychologist James L. Jenkins puts it this way: "If memory is to work well, the rememberer must pick up those aspects of the events or material to be remembered that make possible a well-defined personal experience. For this he needs to be attuned in some way to what is put in front of him."

"Slice of Life," and Analogies

Historically, "slice of life" commercials have always scored high in memorability, and in sales.

They work so well because they help to supply that prior "past experience" that enables a person to better connect with the new information.

Creative people may jeer at those analgesic commercials showing people in pain, but they are going to be remembered.

Analogies also are a powerful way to present a new concept to a prospect. Once again, you're presenting your new idea by associating it with one already lodged in a prospect's mind.

A case in point is the new video service called DBS (Direct Broadcast Satellite). Rather than attempt to explain the technology to intrinsically limited minds, DBS's television commercial presents a simple but powerful analogy:

"Let's say I feel like a movie. Do I drive to a video store? No, I stay right where I am. Direct TV is my video store."

Starting this message with the prospects' existing perception of "video store" is the shortest distance into their minds.

The News Factor

One other way of overcoming the mind's natural stinginess when it comes to accepting new information, is to work hard at presenting your message as important *news*.

Too many advertisements try to entertain or be clever. In so doing they often overlook the news factor in their story.

The Starch research people can demonstrate that headlines that contain news score better in readership than those that don't. Unfortunately, most creative people see this kind of thinking as *old news*.

If people think you've got an important message to convey, generally they'll open their eyes or ears long enough to absorb what you've got to say.

Minds Hate Confusion

Human beings rely more heavily on learning than any other species that has ever existed.

"Learning is the way animals and human beings acquire new information," says a scientist at Columbia University's Center for Neurobiology and Behavior. "Memory is the way they retain that information over time."

"Memory is not just your ability to remember a phone number," says experimental psychologist Lynne Reder, who studied memory at Carnegie-Mellon University. "Rather, it's a dynamic system that's used in every other facet of thought processing. We use memory to see. We use it to understand language. We use it to find our way around."

The Importance of Memory

Another professor of psychology, David Taylor, writes in the British journal *Mind* that

> because our ability to retain information over time is so important, there is a long history of attempts to understand it. Most of these attempts have been based on the idea that there is a place called "memory" in which information is stored for later use.
>
> Explanations of this kind often take the form of an analogy with a physical, external means of storing information. The Greeks, for example, were fond of comparing memory to the

wax tablets that were used for writing in ancient times, whereas contemporary theorists usually refer to the memory systems of computers. Memory has also been compared to a library, a warehouse, and even, albeit with tongue in cheek, a garbage can. The concept of memory as a place has been around for thousands of years, and it forms the basis for most of the explanations of remembering offered by psychologists today.

So if memory is so important, what's the secret of being remembered?

Keep It Simple

When asked what single event was most helpful to him in developing the theory of relativity, Albert Einstein is reported to have answered: "Figuring out how to think about the problem."

John Sculley, former chairman of Apple Computer, put it this way:

> Everything we have learned in the industrial age has tended to create more and more complication. I think that more and more people are learning that you have to simplify, not complicate. That is a very Asian idea—that simplicity is the ultimate sophistication.
>
> Eventually, we will come up with a totally different view of this. The facts won't have changed; it is just that our point of view will have shifted. The development of the Macintosh illustrates this idea. No amount of research would have created the demand for the Macintosh, but once we created it and put it in front of our people, everybody recognized it as something they wanted.

Professional communicators, such as the network broadcasters, understand this principle very well. They keep their word selection very simple.

The Problem of Complexity

We tend to think of boredom as arising from a lack of stimuli. A sort of information *under*load.

But more and more commonly, boredom is arising from excessive stimulation or information overload.

Information, like energy, tends to degrade into entropy— into just noise, redundancy, and banality. To put it another way, the fast horse of information outruns the slow horse of meaning.

Complexity has even overwhelmed people who should know better. *New York Times* editor and author George Johnson writes:

> Neuroscientists—who have seen firsthand the overwhelming complexity of neural tissues—are obsessed with detail and precision. A few neuroscientists, like Nobel Prize–winner John Eccles, have become so impressed by the complications of the brain that they have been reduced to mysticism.

Complexity certainly overwhelmed Hillary Clinton's 1342-page "Health Security Act."

Just look at some of the complicated, confusing, and off-putting ideas in the act: Regional Alliance Health Plans, Premium-Based Financing, Transitional Insurance Reform, Coordination with COBRA Continuation Coverage. It's no wonder America's eyes glazed over.

If Hillary had understood how minds hate confusion, she wouldn't now be reduced to redoing her image into a more traditional mode.

Complicated answers don't help anybody. For instance, every executive wants information, because the difference between a decision and a guess often comes down to information. But today's executives don't want to be buried alive in printouts and reports.

An information clearinghouse named Find/SVP has built a

thriving business in 20 countries, on the premise that less information can be more information. Their researchers are trained to deliver precise but uncomplicated answers. In a few pages, not a few volumes. "Just what you need to know," their slogan says.

Complexity and "More"

We have this terrific word for solving problems: *more.*

When our roads become crowded, we build more roads. When our cities become unsafe, we hire more cops and build more prisons. Whenever our language seems inadequate, we invent more words.

New superhighways relieve the overload of old superhighways, which were built to relieve the overload of highways, which were built to relieve the overload of roads and streets.

This mess can be described as *infinite regress.*

One study has estimated that the average speed on a Los Angeles freeway during rush hour is less than that of a horse and carriage. More roads were supposed to solve the transportation problem. Instead, more roads seem to have brought us nothing but more cars.

"More" doesn't solve the problem. The issue is learning, not schools; safety, not the number of cops; mobility, not highways; performance, not products.

Products with "More"

We have this terrific word for new products: *more.*

Marketing people love to talk about "convergence," the process whereby technologies are merged and wondrous new products are introduced with more and more features. Here's a current sampling:

- AT&T's EO Personal Communicator, a cellular phone, fax, electronic mail, personal organizer, and pen-based computer.

- Okidata's Doc-it, a desktop printer, fax, scanner, and copier.

- Apple's Newton, a fax, beeper, calendar-keeper, and pen-based computer.

- Sony's multimedia player, with display screen and interactive keyboard.

But those are simple compared to Bill Gates' new vision of the wallet of the future. He sees it as a device that will combine or replace keys, charge cards, personal identification, cash, writing implements, a passport, and pictures of the kids. It also would have a global positioning system so you can always tell where you are. (Get lost, Bill.)

Will any of these products make it?

Not likely. They are too confusing and too complex. Most of the world still can't figure out how to record on its VCR.

People resist that which is confusing, and cherish that which is simple. They want to push a button and watch it work.

Confusing Concepts

The basic concept of some products predicts failure. Not because they don't work, but because they don't make sense.

Consider Mennen's Vitamin E deodorant. That's right, you sprayed a vitamin under your arm.

Present this concept to a group of consumers and, guaranteed, you'll get a laugh. It doesn't make sense unless you want the healthiest, best-fed armpits in the nation. No one is going to try to figure *that* one out.

It quickly failed.

Consider Extra-Strength Maalox Whip Antacid. That's right, you sprayed a glob of cream whip on a spoon and took it for your heartburn.

This had a hard time even getting on the shelves, as the druggists laughed the salespeople out of the store. Antacids are tablets or liquids, not whipped cream.

At the time all it did was give the manufacturer, William H. Rorer, a costly case of indigestion.

Confusion strikes again.

More Than People Can Understand

What can a trillion dollars buy that a billion dollars cannot? Numbers are useless unless they can be compared to something you already understand.

For example, Mr. Clinton submitted a 1995 budget of $1.6 trillion. It was a $50 billion increase over the previous year's budget, which was $70 billion more than was spent the year before that.

Yet the budget-busting news was greeted with a yawn of unconcern. Why?

The reason is simple. No one can really cope, mentally, with a number as big as 1,600,000,000,000.

The Wall Street Journal put the amount in some perspective when they presented the budget in these terms:

> If you laid $1 bills from end to end, could you make a chain that stretches to the moon with 1.6 trillion? Answer: without a sweat, with billions and billions of dollars left over. In fact, they would stretch nearly from the Earth to the Sun.

> Imagine a train of 50-foot boxcars crammed with $1 bills. How long would the train have to be to carry the $1.6 trillion Congress spends each year? About $65 million can be stuffed in a boxcar. Thus, the train would have to be about 240 miles long to carry enough dollar bills to balance the federal budget. In other words, you would need a train that stretches the entire Northeast corridor, from Washington, through Baltimore, Delaware, Philadelphia, New Jersey, and into New York City.

Bite-Size Information

This is the approach of *USA Today,* among others. Reduce information into simple, bite-size nuggets.

For instance, how much toothpaste is used in the United States each year? To get the answer, multiply the population (minus the 50 million who are toothless or careless) by the average amount used, which is a half-inch per person per day. Then multiply by 365 days. You come up with an absurdly huge number, about 1.5 million miles of toothpaste. A number that has no real meaning.

So let's look at toothpaste usage in a single day. That comes out to around 3000 miles, about the distance from coast to coast, a distance most people can understand.

If you're trying to communicate a large number, get it down to something that people can get their minds around.

The Power of Oversimplification

The best way to really enter minds that hate complexity and confusion is to oversimplify your message.

In our last book (*The 22 Immutable Laws of Marketing*) we said that some of the most powerful programs are those that focus on a single word. (Crest: *cavities*; Volvo: *safety*; Prego: *thick.*)

AT&T fought back against MCI by planting the word *true* in the minds of its customers and prospects. Who knows what's true or not true about complex long-distance rates? But a little oversimplification can go a long way, when you spend as much money as AT&T. ($500 million.)

Think Simple

The lesson here is not to try to tell your entire story. Just focus on one powerful attribute and drive it into the mind.

That sudden hunch, that creative leap of the mind that "sees" in a flash how to solve a problem in a simple way, is something quite different from general intelligence.

Studies reported in *Scientific American* show that persons with a high "Eureka!" ability are all intelligent to a moderate degree. But beyond that level there seems to be no correlation between high intelligence and the ability to envision simple solutions for complex problems.

If there's any trick to finding that simple set of words, I'd say it's one of being ruthless about how you edit the story you want to tell.

Anything that others could claim just as well as you can, eliminate. Anything that requires a complex analysis to prove, forget. Anything that doesn't fit with your perceptions, avoid.

Finally, never ignore the obvious. Obvious ideas tend to be the most powerful ideas, because they'll be obvious to the market as well.

In fact, most good ideas are obvious in hindsight.

Someone suggests a good idea, a sound strategy, and you wonder, "Why didn't we think of that sooner? It's so obvious."

Author and creativity expert Edward de Bono says it's like climbing a mountain and not seeing the best path until you've reached the top and looked down.

Ideas may seem obvious after the fact. But they weren't obvious to the people who were climbing the mountain.

Minds Are Insecure

A ristotle would have been a lousy ad man. Pure logic is no guarantee of a winning argument.

Minds tend to be emotional, not rational.

Why do people buy what they buy? Why do people act the way they do in the marketplace? According to psychologists Robert Settle and Pamela Alreck, in their book *Why They Buy*, customers don't know, or they won't say.

When you ask people why they made a particular purchase, the responses they give are often not very accurate or useful.

That may mean they really do know, but they're reluctant to tell you the right reason.

More often, they really *don't* know precisely what their own motives are.

Even when it comes to recall, minds are insecure and tend to remember things that no longer exist. Recognition of a well-established brand often stays high over a long time period, even if advertising support is dropped.

In the mid-1980s, an awareness study was conducted on blenders. Consumers were asked to recall all the brand names they could. General Electric came out number two—even though G.E. hadn't made a blender in 20 years.

Buying What Others Buy

Our experience is that people don't know what they want. (So why ask them?)

More times than not, people buy what they think they should have. They're sort of like sheep, following the herd.

Do most people really need a four-wheel-drive vehicle? (No.) If they did, why didn't they become popular years ago? (Not fashionable.)

The main reason for this kind of behavior is insecurity, a subject about which many scientists have written extensively.

Five Forms of Perceived Risk

Minds are insecure for many reasons. One reason is perceived risk in doing something as basic as making a purchase.

Behavioral scientists say there are five forms of perceived risk:

1. Monetary risk. (There's a chance I could lose my money on this.)
2. Functional risk. (Maybe it won't work, or do what it's supposed to do.)
3. Physical risk. (It looks a little dangerous. I could get hurt.)
4. Social risk. (I wonder what my friends will think if I buy this?)
5. Psychological risk. (I might feel guilty or irresponsible if I buy this.)

The Emotional Factor

In his book explaining buyer behavior, Columbia University professor John O'Shaugnessy titles one section "The Importance of Studying Emotion."

In it he writes:

Emotions can activate behavior, provide salience, direct choices, and strengthen other motives. Thus, the social motive to be fashionable is reinforced by pride in exhibiting one's possessions.

Dr. Ernest Dichter, the granddaddy of motivational studies, also writes of emotional and rational behavior:

> Many of our actions are motivated by a conflict between security and change, which often spells insecurity.
>
> There is a silent assumption that rational motivations are somehow more moral, more acceptable than irrational ones. Academic psychology often talks about cognitive versus emotional or affective behavior. I suggest these divisions are wrong and irrelevant.

For example, you might assume that engineers in a large industrial company would absorb information rationally. But when engineers were asked to describe a certain alloy, they offered all kinds of symbolic and allegorical parallels—two metals joining hands, different hot liquids being married in a big vat, etc. (They also provided chemical or mechanical explanations for the alloy.)

Following the Herd

One of the most interesting pieces of work on why people follow the herd was written by Robert Cialdino. He talks of "the principle of social proof" as a potent weapon of influence:

> This principle states that we determine what is correct by finding out what other people think is correct. The principle applies especially to the way we decide what constitutes correct behavior. We view a behavior as correct in a given situation to the degree that we see others performing it.
>
> The tendency to see an action as appropriate when oth-

ers are doing it works quite well normally. As a rule, we will make fewer mistakes by acting in accord with social evidence than by acting contrary to it. Usually, when a lot of people are doing something, it is the right thing to do.

This feature of the principle of social proof is simultaneously its major strength and its major weakness. Like the other weapons of influence, it provides a convenient shortcut for determining the way to behave but, at the same time, makes one who uses the shortcut vulnerable to the attacks of profiteers who lie in wait along its path.

The Testimonial

When people are uncertain, they often will look to others to help them decide how to act.

That's why one of the oldest devices known to advertising man and woman is the testimonial.

A testimonial attacks the insecure mind on several emotional fronts—a trifecta of vanity, jealousy, and fear of being left out.

Stanley Resor, one-time head of J. Walter Thompson, called it "the spirit of emulation." Said Resor: "We want to copy those whom we deem superior in taste or knowledge or experience."

Once upon a time, European opera stars testified to the beneficial effect Lucky Strikes had on their singing. (They sure would sing a different song today.)

The Queen of Rumania said she entrusted her beauty to Pond's cold cream, and her ad in *Ladies' Home Journal* pulled 9400 coupon replies. (Not to be outdone by a foreigner, an ad featuring Mrs. Reginald Vanderbilt drew 10,300 replies.)

"Nine out of ten screen stars," proclaimed a 1927 ad, "care for their skin with Lux toilet soap."

The Bandwagon

Creating a "bandwagon" effect is another powerful technique for dealing with the insecure mind.

Originally, a bandwagon was an elaborately decorated wagon used to transport musicians in a parade. Today it has come to mean any cause or trend that takes an increasing number of people along for the ride.

Polls and panels always make good authority figures to create the bandwagon.

> *Honda Accord:* "In the eight years *Car & Driver* magazine has presented its Ten Best list, only one car has been chosen every time."
>
> *Tylenol:* "Hospitals use Tylenol 18 times more than all ibuprofen brands combined. Tylenol is the pain reliever hospitals use most."
>
> *Crest toothpaste:* "Four out of five dentists surveyed, recommend Crest."
>
> *Canon copiers:* "When it comes to business copiers, the choice is Canon. Number one in copier placements for seven consecutive years."

Another bandwagon strategy for dealing with the insecure mind is that of the "fastest-growing" or "largest-selling." It says that others obviously think we have a pretty good product.

The Heritage

Marketers also display their tradition and culture as a way of getting you on their bandwagon. (After all, how can a mere consumer argue with heritage?)

As early as 1919, a Steinway Piano was being described in an advertisement as "the instrument of the immortals."

More recently, Cross Pen trumpeted its products as "flawless classics, since 1846."

Glenlivet Scotch positions itself as "the father of all Scotch. His Majesty's Government bestowed on The Glenlivet Distillery the very first license under The Act of 1823 to distill single malt whisky in the Highlands."

Coke has exploited its heritage in inventing the cola by calling itself "the real thing." That is their most powerful strategy. "Always Coke" ignores this heritage, and is nothing but wishful thinking. (In reality, half the time, it's always Pepsi.)

Absolut versus Stolichnaya

At present, the battle for the high end of the vodka market is becoming interesting.

Michel Roux, the CEO of Carillon Importers, drove Absolut into the lead with aggressive, highly visual advertising.

Then one day, Michel woke up to find that his nightmare had come true: the right to distribute Absolut had been sold to Seagram.

Undaunted, he started to distribute archrival Stolichnaya. Obviously, his objective was not to get mad, but to get even.

So the battle is on. Will Stoli make an impact and become an "Absolute Pain" for Absolut? Not so far.

A Bad Move

Michel's first move was to employ the strategy that he used to make Absolut famous. He started using Russian art in highly visual advertising. Also there was something about "freedom of vodka."

If you acknowledge that minds are insecure, telling people they have a choice isn't going to have any impact. They really don't know what to choose. After all, we're talking about a substance that by law has to be tasteless and odorless.

And those Russian pictures certainly weren't going to make any difference. So far, it looks like an "Absolut Victory."

Invoke "Heritage"

The only strategy that Stolichnaya should pursue is that of heritage.

They should take advantage of a little-known fact: Absolut is made by a Swedish vodka company.

They should reposition Absolut where it belongs, in Sweden, while they take advantage of their own Russian heritage. The advertisement they should run would have the headline:

"Absolut Sweden vs. Absolute Russian."

Swedish vodka just doesn't sound as good as Russian vodka. Everyone knows that Russian vodka is the real thing.

Now those insecure minds would have a real reason to buy Stolichnaya.

Are you reading, Michel?

Minds Don't Change

The futility of trying to change minds in the marketplace is a lesson we learned many years ago.

Those were the days when we were trying to drag the perceptions of Western Union into the twentieth century.

We tried advertising everything from satellite launches to advanced communications services. Nothing worked.

After years of effort, the consumer's perception of Western Union as the old-fashioned telegraph company was as strong as ever. Our final advice: Change the company name to Westar, and use the Western Union brand only on the telegraph and money-order services. Anything else was hopeless.

While the advice was good, our message wasn't well received.

Expensive Failures to Change Minds

Since that time, we've watched many others blow a lot of money on trying to change minds in the marketplace.

Xerox lost hundreds of millions trying to convince the market that Xerox machines that didn't make copies were worth the money.

No one would buy their computers.

Volkswagen dropped over 60 share points, trying to convince the market that VW wasn't just a small, reliable, economical car like the Beetle.

No one bought their big, fast cars.

Coca-Cola blew both prestige and money in an effort to convince the market they had a better thing than the Real Thing.

No one bought their New Coke.

When the market makes up its mind about a product, there's no changing that mind.

Most people think Japanese electronics are superior.

So when researchers put a Sanyo label on an RCA home electronics device, they asked 900 people to compare its performance to the same product with the RCA label. Seventy-six percent said the Sanyo product was better.

As John Kenneth Galbraith once said: "Faced with the choice between changing one's mind and proving that there is no need to do so, almost everyone gets busy on the proof."

Minds Are Hard to Change

A general feeling in the marketing industry has always been that new-product advertising should generate higher interest than advertising for established brands.

But it turns out that we're actually more impressed by what we already know (or buy) than by what's "new."

One research organization, McCollum Spielman, has tested more than 22,000 TV commercials over 23 years. Almost 6000 of those commercials were for new products in 10 product categories.

What did they learn? Greater persuasion ability and attitude shifts—the so-called "new-product excitement"—were evident in only *one* of the 10 categories (pet products) when comparing new brands to established brands.

In the other nine categories—ranging from drugs to beverages to personal hygiene items—there was no real difference, no burst of excitement, enabling consumers to distinguish between established brands and new brands.

With thousands of different commercials across hundreds of different brands, you can pretty much rule out "creativity" as the difference in persuasion. It comes back to what we're familiar with, what we're already comfortable with.

Trying to Change Attitudes

In the book *The Reengineering Revolution*, MIT professor-turned-consultant Michael Hammer calls human beings' innate resistance to change "the most perplexing, annoying, distressing, and confusing part" of reengineering.

To help us better understand this resistance, a book entitled *Attitudes & Persuasion* offers some insights. Written by Richard Petty and John Cacioppo, it spends some time on "belief systems." Here's their take on why minds are so hard to change:

> The nature and structure of belief systems is important from the perspective of an informational theorist, because beliefs are thought to provide the cognitive foundation of an attitude.
>
> In order to change an attitude, then, it is presumably necessary to modify the information on which that attitude rests. It is generally necessary, therefore, to change a person's beliefs, eliminate old beliefs, or introduce new beliefs.

And you're going to do all that with a 30-second commercial?

What Psychologists Say

The Handbook of Social Psychology reinforces how tough it is to change attitudes:

> Any program to change attitudes offers formidable problems. The difficulty of changing a person's basic beliefs,

even through so elaborate and intense a procedure as psychotherapy, becomes understandable, as does the fact that procedures that are effective in changing some attitudes have little effect on others.

And what makes things even worse is that *truth* has no real bearing on these issues. Check out this observation:

People have attitudes on a staggeringly wide range of issues. They seem to know what they like (and especially dislike) even regarding objects about which they know little, such as Turks, or which have little relevance to their daily concerns, like life in outer space.

So, to paraphrase an old TV show, if your assignment, Mr. Phelps, is to change people's minds, don't accept the assignment.

Reclaiming Old Ideas

Interestingly, many marketers are utilizing the mind's unwillingness to change to their advantage. Their premise: If it's difficult to change a mind, then it's easy to go back and reclaim an old idea.

That's consistent with new studies from the Pennsylvania Medical Center. Neurologists there claim the most durable form of memory is located in a part of the brain you've never heard of (the angular gyrus).

They call it "semantic memory"—the memory of what words and symbols mean. The memory of what distinguishes a dog from a cat resides here. So does Speedy Alka-Seltzer and Maytag's lonely repairman.

One study of brand-name familiarity supported this premise. It asked housewives in four cities to name as many brands as they could. They were paid for each name. They mentioned a total of 4900 brands, according to the *Journal of Marketing Research*. (Money talks.)

The age of these remembered brand names was remarkable. More than 85 percent of them had been around for 25 years or more.

Maybe that's why more and more marketers are "going back" to reclaim old ideas and old messages. This isn't nostalgia for the sake of nostalgia. It's marketing that reclaims ideas that still belong to you.

One psychologist who studies advertising says that this strategy of looking to a product's heritage for a new marketing campaign is virtually risk-free: "It suggests history and endurance for a product. It gives a sense that a product has roots. And there is a collective cultural identity. It triggers bonding between the consumer and the company."

Says an identity consultant: "It breaks through the clutter. Many consumers are already familiar with the icon or the old campaign, so the company doesn't have to work hard to establish itself in their minds. The consumer doesn't have to take too many mental steps."

A researcher says that by running a 30-year-old campaign, you reinforce your durability. It sets an aura around the product. It says, "We've been around for a long time, and we know what we're talking about."

Says the president of J.B. Williams Co. (owner of the Brylcreem, Aqua Velva, and Lectric Shave brands): "There's a franchise there that even neglect couldn't destroy."

Some Current "Reclaiming" Programs

So everything old is new again. Here's a sampling of nostalgia now being used in marketing land:

- KFC has resurrected Col. Harland Sanders in its advertising. (The actual colonel died in 1980. An actor now appears in new black-and-white footage.)
- Timex tried to convince the market that it sells fashionable

watches, but with no success. It's back to what people remember: "It takes a licking, and keeps on ticking."

- Campbell Soup tried to convince the market that "Soup is good food." The market said "Soup is soup." Now they're back with the classic "Mmm Mmm! Good!"

- Ford is slipping footage of the 1965 Mustang into commercials for their new models. Today the old Mustang is a classic, a bigger deal than it was back then.

- Shake 'N Bake has brought back its little girl ("And I helped") from the 1960s. Marketing executives say that it breaks through the clutter.

- Brylcreem has reprised its memorable line: "A little dab'll do ya." Don La Rosa, president, says the company is trying to tap and build on the equity the advertising has accrued over decades.

- Foster Grant has revised its "Who's behind those Foster Grants?" with a new series of celebrities on the rise. (In your face, Ralph Lauren.)

The Porsche Comeback

And we're not just talking about advertising ideas. You can do the same with products.

Porsche has recently come back from a near-death experience. In 1986, they sold 30,000 cars in the U.S. market. By 1993 they were down to 3700 cars, and losing a lot of money.

Their problem, as we saw it, was that they had drifted away from what they were in the mind, the 911 Carrera. (The rear-engine, air-cooled, six-cylinder car.)

Then they tried to convince the market that a Porsche wasn't just the 911. It was also the 968 (front-engine, water-cooled, four cylinders) as well as the 928 (mid-engine, water-cooled, eight cylinders).

So what was the Porsche? It was a front/rear, air/water, 4/6/8–cylinder, cheap expensive car. (They lost focus. See the next chapter.)

So what did they do? They went back and reclaimed their old identity, with an updated and less expensive version of their popular Carrera 911.

Today, sales are up more than 50 percent in the U.S. market, thanks to—you guessed it—the 911.

This same strategy would work for Volkswagen. If they were to bring back the Beetle in a new form, it would be a howling success. Because that small, reliable, economical car lingers on in the mind as what VW is all about.

Yes, Virginia, you *can* go back. Because minds don't change.

Minds Can Lose Focus

In days gone by, most big brands were clearly perceived by their customers. The mind, like a camera, had a very clear picture of what its favorite brands were all about.

When Anheuser-Busch proudly proclaimed that "This Bud's For You!" the customer knew exactly what was being served.

The same went for Miller High Life, or plain old Coors Beer.

But in the past decade, Budweiser has brought out 15 new products. Miller and Coors checked in with 14 and 11 new offerings respectively.

The market has been flooded with regulars, lights, drafts, clears, cold-brewed, dry-brewed, and ice-brewed beers.

Now the statement "This Bud's for you" can only elicit the question, "Which one do you have in mind?"

That clear perception in the mind is now badly out of focus. It's no wonder the King of Beers is starting to lose its following.

The Line Extension Trap

Loss of focus is really all about line extension. And no issue in marketing is so controversial.

In our 1972 *Advertising Age* articles, we cautioned companies not to fall into what we called "the line extension trap."

Positioning: The Battle for Your Mind contains two chapters on the problem of line extension.

In *The 22 Immutable Laws of Marketing,* it became our single most violated law.

Not that our lack of approval has slowed anyone down. In fact, quite the opposite has been true. "Extending brand equity" has become all the rage, as companies like Coca-Cola talk about concepts such as "megabrands."

For years we were the lonely voices railing against line extension. Even the *Journal of Consumer Marketing* noticed this: "Ries and Trout stand alone as the only outright critics of the practice of brand extension." (Our minds don't change.)

That's until recently when the *Harvard Business Review* rendered their verdict: "Unchecked product-line expansion can weaken a brand's image, disturb trade relations, and disguise cost increases."

Keep it up, guys.

A Matter of Perspective

The difference in views on this subject is essentially a perspective. Companies look at their brands from an economic point of view. To gain cost efficiencies and trade acceptance, they are quite willing to turn a highly focused brand, one that stands for a certain type of product or idea, into an unfocused brand that represents two or three or more types of products or ideas.

We look at the issue of line extension from the point of view of the mind. The more variations you attach to the brand, the more the mind loses focus. Gradually, a brand like Chevrolet comes to mean nothing at all.

Scott, the leading brand of toilet tissue, line-extended its name into Scotties, Scottkins, Scotttowels. Pretty soon "Scott" flunked the shopping-list test. (You can't write down "Scott" and have it mean anything.)

Danger: A Well-Focused Specialist

Things would have been fine in the land of Scott if the likes of Mr. Whipple and his squeezeable Charmin tissue hadn't arrived on the scene. (The more you lose focus, the more vulnerable you become.) It didn't take long for Charmin to become the number-one tissue.

The course of recent business history seems to verify our concerns.

For years, Procter & Gamble's Crisco brand was the leading shortening. Then the world turned to vegetable oil. Of course, Procter & Gamble turned to Crisco Oil.

So who's the winner in the vegetable oil war? Wesson, of course.

Time moves on, and corn oil appears on the scene. Of course, Wesson keeps up with technology by introducing Wesson Corn Oil.

So who's the big winner in the corn-oil melee? That's right, Mazola.

The success of a no-cholesterol corn oil suggests a no-cholesterol-corn-oil margarine. So Mazola introduces Mazola Corn Oil Margarine.

So who's the winner in the corn-oil-margarine category? You're right, it's Fleischmann's.

In each case, the specialist or the well-focused competitor was the winner.

Some Surprising Research

With about 70 percent of new products being launched with existing brand names, you would think these companies would have some supporting data on the pluses of line extension.

The opposite is true.

The *Journal of Consumer Marketing* also noted that

Nielsen conducted a large-scale study of 115 new-product launches across five U.S. and U.K. markets. The study compared the market share gained by products launched under established family or corporate brand names with market share gained by products launched with new brand names. Share was measured two years after each brand's launch. The brand extensions performed significantly less well than the products launched with new brand names.

Some Surprising Numbers

To support this point, some numbers might be in order. In 1979, the Miller High Life and Miller Light brands totaled 35 million barrels in sales. The basic Budweiser brand sold 30 million barrels.

By 1990, Miller had added Genuine Draft to its lineup. Their three brands sold 32 million barrels. That's right, three million *less*. Meanwhile the regular Budweiser had risen to 50 million barrels.

You would have thought that Miller's declining numbers would have sent a negative message about line extension to Anheuser Busch. Wrong. Budweiser went the way of Miller and started adding other Budweiser brands (Light, Dry, Ice, etc.).

The result: The Budweiser brand has slid from 50 million to 43 million barrels. More brands, less focus, less sales.

Another study compared the survival rates (after six years) of 84 new, nondurable consumer products. It found no significant difference between the survival rates of the brand extensions and the new-brand launches.

This evidence suggests that brand extension gives little advantage to a new-product release. It is particularly disconcerting when the inherent disadvantages of brand extension are considered.

The Spillover Problem

There's also a rarely discussed dark side of line extension.

The continued practice of brand extension exposes a greater range of brands to the possible spillover of negative publicity. Bad publicity for one brand may spill over to other brands sharing the brand name.

In Australia, Colgate-Palmolive suffered the consequences of having its family name on nearly every one of its vast array of brands, after a highly publicized extortion attempt involving cyanide contamination.

The Specialist's Weapons

Here are some thoughts on why the specialist brand appears to make such an impression on the mind.

First, the specialist can focus on one product, one benefit, one message. This focus enables the marketer to put a sharp point on the message that quickly drives it into the mind. Some examples: Domino's Pizza can focus on its home delivery. Pizza Hut has to talk about *both* home delivery and sit-down service.

Duracell can focus on longlasting alkaline batteries. Eveready had to talk about flashlight, heavy-duty, rechargeable, and alkaline batteries. (Then they got smart and went to the Energizer only, a good move on Eveready's part.)

Castrol can focus on its oil for high-performance small engines. Pennzoil and Quaker State are marketed for all types of engines.

Another weapon of the specialist is the ability to be perceived as the expert or the best. Cray is the best in super-computers. Philadelphia is the best cream cheese. (The original, so to speak.)

Finally, the specialist can become the "generic" for the category. Xerox became the generic word for copying. ("Please Xerox that for me.")

Federal Express became the generic word for overnight delivery. ("I'll FedEx it to you.")

3M's Scotch tape became the generic word for cellophane tape. ("I'll Scotch-tape it together.")

Even though the lawyers hate it, making the brand name a generic is the ultimate weapon in the marketing wars. But it's something only a specialist can do. The generalist can't become a generic.

Nobody ever says, "Get me a beer from the G.E."

The Levi Lesson

No company better understands the problems of line extension and lack of focus than Levi Strauss & Co., the fabled maker of jeans.

In the 1970s and early 1980s they tried "extending the equity of the brand" with reckless abandon.

They of course had their jeans. But sensing a trend toward more casualwear, they also launched Levi's Casuals and Levi's Chinos. Then for good measure (or bad measure), they launched Levi's for the Feet.

In an attempt to attack the dress-up market, Levi Strauss & Co. introduced Levi's Pantela Sportswear, Levi's Tailored Classics, and Levi's Action Slacks and Suits.

It all became a Levi's too far. Confusion reigned. And the perceptions of *denim, durable,* and *workingmen* got in the way of what the casualwear buyer was after.

A New Brand

Finally, a team of people from Levi's Menswear refocused the company back on what they called their "core competencies." While the jeans division concentrated on what it did best, making denim jeans, Levi's Menswear Division developed a new brand called Dockers.

The Dockers line of products was targeted at the 25- to 45-year-old Baby Boomers who had grown up wearing Levi's jeans. With a skosh more room, an upscale image, and a non-denim brand name, they were ready to sail. And sail they did, as Dockers became a billion-dollar business.

Today, Levi's jeans are a multibillion-dollar global business, and Dockers is the number-one-selling pant in America. (Dockers have been so successful, in fact, that the company has launched the brand in Sweden, Germany, and other parts of Europe.)

Pretty impressive, for a company that used to sell a few hundred pairs a year to miners in the California Gold Rush of the 1850s!

You might say the real gold wasn't in the hills. It was in the pants.

PART TWO

Dealing with Change

To survive, to avert what we have termed future shock, the individual must become infinitely more adaptable and capable than ever before.

ALVIN TOFFLER
Future Shock

Repositioning: Where Positioning Is At

These are the times that try a business person's soul.

Alvin Toffler once wrote a famous book called *Future Shock*. Its premise was that ever-accelerating change would have a shocking effect on people.

Time has proven his predictions to be very accurate. But what he left out was the impact on *corporations* of accelerating change. It has been just as traumatic.

Some of America's biggest and most successful companies have been challenged or even brought to their knees by change. General Motors, IBM, Sears Roebuck, Westinghouse, Digital Equipment, Wang, Kodak—the list goes on and on.

Losing Sight of Change

Companies that lose sight of their markets quickly suffer the consequences. Today, the danger of losing market position is especially great. The four primary reasons for this are

1. The fast pace of changing technology
2. The quick and unpredictable shifting of consumer attitudes
3. The increase in competition within the global economy

4. The increase in competition among creative executives in U.S. companies (They're getting good at this competitive stuff.)

It's a time not so much for positioning as for *repositioning*. (In 1994, this word was mentioned 5155 times in U.S. business publications.)

GM's Sad Saga

Consider the plight of General Motors. In 1921, Alfred P. Sloan, Jr. arrived and found seven brands of automobiles all competing in the middle of the market. Their average selling price was about $1200. Brilliantly, he eliminated two and repositioned the remaining brands along different price points:

Chevrolet..................... $450 to $600

Pontiac.........................$600 to $900

Oldsmobile................. $900 to $1,200

Buick.........................$1,200 to $1,700

Cadillac................... $1,700 to $2,500

It was an enormous success, and over the years these five brands drove up GM's market share to close to 50 percent of the business.

But they couldn't keep Alfred propped up forever. Eventually he died, and the accountants took over. With his hands off the steering wheel, these five brands all rushed to the center of the market. Each brand lost its focus or position.

In many ways they all went right back to 1921, as today's prices look like this:

Saturn......................$9,995 to $12,895

Chevrolet................. $7,295 to $67,543

Pontiac.....................$9,904 to $26,479	
Oldsmobile..............$13,510 to $31,370	
Buick..................... $13,734 to $31,864	
Cadillac..................$32,990 to $45,330	

With the exception of Saturn and Cadillac they all are back in the middle, trying to be everything to everyone.

And on top of *pricing* all their cars alike, they tended to make them all *look* alike. (A nice money-saving idea.) It's no wonder General Motors has lost 11 points of market share over the past decade. It's also not surprising that the board revolted and ejected the top management.

The job ahead for General Motors? To reposition all their brands. (Where's Mr. Sloan now that they need him?)

As this book goes to press, a new marketing shooter named Ron Zarrella has arrived at GM to rethink the brands. With the kind of internal politics he'll encounter, Mr. Zarrella had better keep his back to a wall at all times.

Back to Basics

In almost every issue of the business press, you read about companies "getting back to basics." Sears divested its Allstate Insurance Company, sold Sears Tower, and shed all of its financial services subsidiaries. It also closed its catalog operation. The result: Retailing earnings for 1994 were up 30 percent over 1993.

Xerox was once positioned as the plain-paper copier. Then they decided to pursue computers, with disastrous results. Now they're repositioning themselves as "the Document Company."

Mead Corporation has spun off its very successful Lexis/Nexis business to reposition themselves back to paper products.

Quaker Oats, General Mills, and Procter & Gamble are focusing on their core brands. Marlboro is back in Marlboro Country. (After finally realizing that real cowboys don't smoke menthols or mediums.)

Kodak also is repositioning itself on film, and selling off many of its nonphotographic units.

The problems that many of these companies encountered were located not in their plans but in the minds of their prospects. Consumers expect companies to be specialists in narrow fields, especially when a business has carved out a strong niche and achieved name recognition. For the same reason, consumers become suspicious when the field widens.

Usually their suspicions are justified, because products in different markets are rarely as good as the original product—which has been honed and perfected over many years. Not only is money wasted on expansion, but market share for their original product slips. Fortunately, Xerox had the fiscal and management resources to correct its error. At great expense, it went back to basics and repositioned itself on plain-paper copiers. It succeeded in regaining market share.

Avoiding Costly Mistakes

There is no reason why any company should have to pay for such an expensive lesson. It must stay in touch with the marketplace and have the courage to reposition itself before the company's products, image, and revenue have greatly suffered.

Positioning is simply concentrating on an idea—or even a word—that defines the company in the minds of consumers. Having a strong brand identification gives a company an immense edge. It's more efficient to market one successful concept to one large group of people, than 50 product or service ideas under the same brand to 50 separate groups.

Consider the trials and tribulations undergone by two Japanese car manufacturers. As a result both of a lack of focus and of the ill-fated Joe Isuzu program, the Isuzu car company had losses of over $400 million in 1992. Then they had the courage to reposition themselves. Today they are profitable, and can't make enough of these vehicles. (See Chapter 16.)

Subaru did the opposite. Infected by the "me-too" spirit, they moved their focus away from their rugged four-wheel-drive cars and added a car line. This idea was supported by advertising that said "a car is a car." Subaru has been struggling ever since.

To avoid making a similar mistake, a company must constantly survey their customers. They should ask questions that let customers articulate their concept of the company's product or service. If it's not the same as the *company's* concept, that company is headed for trouble.

When consumers are asked for their impressions of Volvo cars, they reply in terms of safety. That's the perception that Volvo owns in the mind. So who was first to offer side-impact air bags, a new safety feature? Volvo, reinforcing their safety perception. On the other hand, consumers have a tough time defining Chevrolet.

Think Small and Don't Tinker

Monitor technology and product innovations. The best way to peer into future markets is to watch small companies. IBM should have been watching companies such as Apple and Tandy in the early 1980s. If it had been, it would have learned that PCs would soon capture a large share of the computer market.

Keep company managers from going off in unfocused directions. It's often the most creative people who love to tinker and think of new products and new twists for existing ones. But unless these ideas are consistent with the consumer's concepts and the company's track record of success, they are sure to nudge the company out of focus or position in the mind. Volvo could easily build a sports car, but that would abruptly bring it out of focus as a brand identified with safety.

When the Market Changes

Repositioning is a must when customer attitudes have changed, technology has overtaken existing products, and products have strayed away from the consumer's long-standing perception of them.

Consider America's attitude change about red meat. In 1986, beef consumption was 74 pounds per person. By 1990, it had fallen to 64 pounds per person.

During the same time period, chicken consumption climbed from 44 pounds per person to 49 pounds per person.

This attitude change did not go unnoticed by the pork industry as they repositioned pork as "The Other White Meat." (If you can't fight them, join them.)

Today's computer marketplace has moved from "proprietary" to "open" software. IBM, which made its name and money on proprietary software, must reposition itself so as to accommodate this shift in customer attitudes. That's exactly what they *aren't* doing, as they continue to push their "proprietary" OS/2 against Microsoft's "open" Windows software.

All of these decisions are tough for a company to come to terms with. But not making the correct decision at the appropriate time can be devastating to a company's future.

In today's hostile market, it is increasingly important not only to be up-to-date with one's own company, but also to be intimately knowledgeable about one's competition. As companies look toward the next century, managers must have the courage to make the types of decisions that companies like Xerox, Volvo, and Lotus have made. If they don't, they will suffer the consequences.

The stories in the following chapters should help you to better understand the repositioning process, and how to pursue it.

Repositioning a Software Company

As markets mature and technology changes, there are times when a company requires new focus that will better suit them in the future.

Changing focus in mid-market is one of the trickiest maneuvers in marketing, as your timing must be exquisite. First you must delicately balance your internal resources, as you shift. Then you must figure out how you slow down support for the original business, while you use resources to ramp up your business of the future. Then comes the real work: dealing with all the internal egos who see their future threatened.

No better case study illustrates this kind of situation than that of Lotus Development Corporation, the company that brought the world the spreadsheet.

The Going Gets Tough

The world turns quickly, in high-tech land. In the mid-eighties, new spreadsheet competition arrived and margins started to tighten up. Borland entered the fray with a good product and very aggressive pricing. If that wasn't bad enough, Microsoft, the 800-pound software gorilla, arrived with a new operating system called Windows. Then they carefully designed their Excel spreadsheet product around this new operating system.

When the dust had settled, Excel was the preferred Windows spreadsheet product, and it was trench warfare in spreadsheet land. Alas for Lotus, it was time to think about moving on, or as we like to say, *shifting the battlefield.*

Early Efforts

The first efforts to move beyond the spreadsheet were purchases of other types of software, such as word-processing and graphics. But two problems haunted Lotus. Other products already dominated these categories. And Lotus made name assumptions that weren't accurate.

Management assumed the company name to be Lotus and the brand name to be "1-2-3." And with this assumption in hand, they continued the pattern of naming.

They presented Lotus as a company with other brands such as Improv, Ami Pro, Freelance, Notes, and Symphony. (As well as 1-2-3.)

This made eminent sense inside Lotus. But the real question is whether this made sense in the minds of their prospects in the marketplace.

Needed: A Big Name

The name reality is that in the mind they don't have a big company name like IBM or Microsoft.

What they really have is one big brand name, Lotus 1-2-3.

This is the case for a very practical and simple reason. In the mind, numbers can't stand alone. People don't think in numbers, they think in words. "500SL" and "914" and "1-2-3" all have to be connected to a name if they are to register in the mind. You see, numbers conjure up a name. It's a Mercedes-Benz 500 SL. It's a Xerox 914. It's Lotus 1-2-3.

Sure, you'll use the numbers as a nickname, but you can

do this only when you have locked the name that goes with the numbers into your mind.

And it's not like Lotus wasn't encouraging the connection. They sure were.

Advertising featuring the "Lotus Spreadsheet Family" continued to lock "Lotus" and "Spreadsheet" together in the mind.

But if they wanted to go beyond 1-2-3, Lotus needed a different corporate name to put at the bottom of their ads.

Our recommendation is to use their real name: Lotus Development Corporation. Right off the bat it sounds more impressive. It also implies that they're developing other types of products beyond their spreadsheet.

Needed: A New Idea

While that move was an option, what was the big new idea they could focus on? Better software?

In combing through the material gathered on our visit to their offices in Cambridge, we came across a very interesting *Business Week* article. It talked about how software is changing, and how networks of computers are taking over. Result: new products on the horizon for companies like Lotus Development Corp.

The key message in this article was that the future belongs to the PC Network. That's the new game in town. And with Notes, Lotus was reported to be on the leading edge of this new trend.

But also in this article there appeared one word that we thought could be Lotus's next *spreadsheet*.

The word or concept was *groupware*. This is a natural way to describe software for network applications. (Groups of computers.)

We suspected they could jump on this word and make it their own, just as they had been able to preempt the word *spreadsheet*. The reason was that Lotus had the credentials.

Their Notes product was billed by *Business Week* as the first successful groupware program. And given their technological lead, they had some running room to preempt the "groupware" concept.

For those not familiar with Notes, this product took 15 tough years to develop. The key feature is its ability to "replicate" whatever is inputted around the network. If a document is changed in one place, it's changed everywhere. Believe me, that's no easy task. Just ask Microsoft, a company that's been trying to replicate this process for years.

Connecting Perceptions

In the process of repositioning, it can be very helpful if you can find a way to connect to what is already in the mind as a starting point for your message. (A mental shortcut, so to speak.)

Since "spreadsheet" represented Lotus in the mind, we saw that as being the natural starting point for the repositioning process. In simple and direct terms, the repositioning message that should be developed to their customers and prospects should look and sound like this:

Lotus Development Corp.
First the spreadsheet.
Now groupware.

Nothing cute. Just tell it like it is.

Off to the Races

And indeed, groupware became the focus as Jim Manzi, the CEO, began the process of building and supporting the Notes Groupware business.

In 1990, they had only 70 customers using this software. In

1991, there were 400. In 1992, 1400 had signed on. In 1993, 3200, and in 1994 there were 5000 organizations using Notes.

That's about 7 million computers, now using groupware as a way to enhance corporate togetherness.

Even more startling is the shrinking amount of time it now takes to deploy this software in an organization. In 1991 it took about 19 months. In 1994 the time was down to less than *three* months.

Also, to accelerate the process, Lotus signed up 8000 partners that are now installing and programming Notes applications for companies around the world.

But don't let all those numbers lull you into thinking it was easy.

Internal Struggle

Getting to where Lotus is positioned today took an enormous effort on the part of CEO Jim Manzi.

When asked about this effort of changing focus, he summed it up as "a brutal process." Here is the story in his own words:

> The spreadsheet was the center of gravity at Lotus. It once represented 70 percent of our business. It was our "mainframe" business, so to speak. But Microsoft and Windows really put a big hole in our future.
>
> In the early nineties I felt Notes was the best future we had. Unfortunately, not everyone in the company felt that way. Many wanted to just continue to improve the spreadsheet. During one difficult period, twelve VPs left the company. They didn't see the future the way I did.
>
> All this, plus the ongoing investment in this product, didn't go unnoticed by our Board of Directors. Keeping them on the Notes bandwagon required telling the story over and over, maintaining perspective, and building relationships

both inside and outside the company. Once the Board loses that vision of the future, your problems magnify.

Luckily the numbers started to get better and people started to get more comfortable with an investment that is closing in on $500 million.

Hey, I never said that repositioning was simple or inexpensive. But as *Fortune* magazine reported: "In groupware, Lotus Development rules. Its product, Lotus Notes, is fast becoming for computer networks what Lotus 1-2-3 was for PCs."

It looks like Jim Manzi's vision is about to pay off. As this book goes to press, IBM just agreed to pay $3.5 billion for Lotus. Big Blue must see groupware as a big winner.

THE LESSON

The Lotus story clearly points to the need for a CEO to get emotionally involved in the repositioning process. Only the CEO can keep the vision intact. Only the CEO can resolve the conflicts that will arise. Only the CEO can keep the Board from sidetracking the strategy before it has had time to begin to show results.

NINE

Repositioning an Ice Cream Company

Time and competition march on relentlessly. And no company has been buffeted by these two forces more than an ice cream company called Carvel. But first, a little history.

In 1936, a refrigeration expert named Tom Carvel was an early pioneer in the field of soft ice cream. Being first is important, but the trick is to exploit your "first-ness" while the exploiting is good. You've got to go nationwide before your competition can gain strength.

As it turned out, a better name for the product would have been *fresh* ice cream. (As in fresh orange juice, fresh ham, etc.)

Even today, almost 60 years later, people are still confused. Many think that soft ice cream is a different kind of ice cream, rather than fresh ice cream before it is frozen.

Enter the Competitors

In 1944, Dairy Queen arrived on the scene, and soft ice cream competition was born. That wasn't a problem. A competitor or two or three usually adds credibility to the category, which tends to broaden the market rather than hurt the pioneer. After all, to be a leader you have to have followers.

In the 1950s more competition arrived, in the form of Tastee Freeze and Mister Softee. Now the soft-ice-cream wars were really under way. The existence of *four* competitors makes things a lot more uncomfortable than just two or three. It was time to do something to strengthen Carvel's position.

Tom Carvel made a brilliant move in the 1950s, when he introduced franchising. This is an excellent way to broaden one's base. Alas, he should have done it a decade or so earlier, when he still had a clear field.

The race was over, as the nationwide soft-ice-cream winner was Dairy Queen. Carvel had been overtaken in the race for leadership in the category.

This may have disheartened Tom, but it didn't slow him down.

Moving to Cakes

Carvel started to line-extend beyond soft ice cream to hard ice cream, cakes, novelties, and frozen yogurt. Unfortunately this effort didn't dramatically help things, as new competition continued to arrive in all ice cream categories. Häagen Dazs in premium, Baskin-Robbins with flavors, Ben & Jerry with toppings, and more recently, TCBY in frozen yogurt.

Beyond the problem of competition, a larger one began to threaten Carvel.

Loss of Focus

The Carvel chain had lost its focus, as franchisees began to go their own way. One store proclaimed itself an "ice cream supermarket." Trying to be all things to all people is never a good strategy. Today the marketing wars are being won by the well-focused specialists.

Obviously, a repositioning strategy was needed. Should Carvel do what others had done, go back to the basics of soft ice cream? As we began to look at this problem, we weren't so sure they had any place to go back to.

The problem was that, with the arrival of frozen yogurt, even the concept of soft ice cream had lost its focus. More and more, people were perceiving "frozen yogurt" as an attractive, low-calorie alternative to soft ice cream.

Nothing dramatized this better than the success of TCBY (The Country's Best Yogurt) and others.

Everyone into Yogurt

Even the long-time leader in premium ice cream had added frozen yogurt. Some stores were doing 40 percent of their business in frozen yogurt.

Everyone was jumping on the bandwagon.

Baskin-Robbins changed its name from Baskin-Robbins Ice Cream to Baskin-Robbins Ice Cream & Frozen Yogurt. Meanwhile the Carvel stores were heavily promoting Lo-Yo, their own frozen yogurt.

Frozen yogurt is in the process of replacing soft ice cream, in much the same way as Advil is slowly replacing Tylenol.

As we saw it, frozen yogurt is the main reason Carvel can't go home to soft ice cream. What was called for was a repositioning strategy based on a new concept with a future.

What's Carvel in the Mind?

We combed their research to see what perceptions of Carvel the public had in its mind.

Respondents said that Carvel reminds them of their childhood. It brings back memories of when they were kids. Plus, Carvel is perceived as having been in business a long time.

Unfortunately, all this nostalgia only tended to make them appear "old-fashioned."

Carvel also was perceived as being "soft and fresh." Respondents say that Carvel has a soft-ice-cream machine. You can see the employees making ice cream, and it has ice cream made fresh daily at the store.

But as we said, a focus on "soft" wouldn't be very productive in this age of frozen yogurt.

Carvel also was perceived as "value." Some respondents in the research said that Carvel has the lowest prices; it's good value for the money, and it offers a lot of price coupons.

Value is certainly a good perception to have, especially in a recession economy. It certainly made Taco Bell the big chain it is today.

But you need more than value alone. Taco Bell, for example, is widely perceived as being the leader in Mexican food.

A New Position Emerges

Carvel also was perceived as "cakes and novelties." Respondents gave the company high marks for having lots of ice cream novelties to choose from. They also were perceived as making their ice cream cakes fresh every day, and having ice cream or frozen yogurt novelties packaged to take home.

Now this was a possible focus, especially when overlaid with another piece of competitive research.

When people were asked who makes ice cream cakes fresh every day, Carvel had a considerable lead over their competitors: 64 percent named Carvel, 40 percent named Baskin-Robbins, 31 percent named Häagen Dazs and 31 percent named TCBY.

This research led us to our repositioning recommendation of shifting the focus from "soft" to "ice cream cakes." The concept: "Carvel, the ice cream bakery."

Interestingly, this wasn't really our own idea, but had been suggested to us by Syl Sosnowski, their head of marketing. But as soon as we heard it, we loved it. We saw the cake focus as taking advantage of public perceptions, while providing a powerful concept to drive the Carvel brand. But this recommendation came with some bad news and some good news.

The bad news was that to execute the cake strategy would require extensive modification of the stores. Carvel would have to be made to look more like a bakery than an ice cream store.

The good news was that redoing the stores to give them a cake focus would help to dispel Carvel's "old-fashioned" perception. Carvel would do away with a negative perception on their way to building a more powerful new-and-improved perception.

Another benefit of the change was that the public's perception of "value" would be much more beneficial to a cake position than to a soft-ice-cream position. While the price of a soft ice cream cone is no big deal, the price of a cake is another matter. Here price does make a difference.

Ice Cream Bakeries Are Founded

Carvel has moved quickly to implement this repositioning strategy on the East Coast. The old Carvel signs are gone, and new "Ice Cream Bakery" graphics have replaced them. But simply replacing a sign doesn't ensure a happy ending to this repositioning story.

First, there's the problem of volume. Can all of their repositioned stores find happiness selling cakes and novelties? Can they generate enough volume to pay for the kind of advertising Carvel needs to build the market for ice cream cakes?

Not likely.

What about opening more bakeries? There certainly isn't a Carvel Ice Cream Bakery in every neighborhood. In this highly competitive world, out of sight sure does mean out of mind.

This also isn't a very likely approach, as specialty ice cream stores are on the decline. Today over half of all ice cream sales have moved to the supermarket.

Going to the Supermarket

This trend has led Carvel to begin to think like a large bakery such as Entenmann's.

They have set up colorful "Ice Cream Bakery" displays in supermarkets, and begun to dramatically widen the availability of their ice cream cakes and novelties. Today 1500 supermarkets are served by the Carvel stores, which have become ice-cream-cake wholesalers.

This makes the important point that rethinking always comes with repositioning. Normally, you can't do things the same old way. You have to be willing to change the company to better line it up with your new position.

A Big Problem Unsolved

Carvel research shows that in terms of awareness of Carvel products, the big winners are special-occasion cakes. Most people think of ice cream cakes only at the approach of a birthday or Mother's Day.

Since such events happen only once a year, ice cream cakes aren't going to fly off those supermarket shelves. This means that Carvel's cakes have to be repositioned as every-day cakes, against the likes of Entenmann's. And to date, I've seen no effective strategy against the everyday-cake crowd.

This also points to another aspect of repositioning. Often, arriving at a new position means gaining a new enemy. In the old days it was soft ice cream versus hard ice cream. For an "ice cream bakery," it's ice cream cakes versus cake cakes.

Our advice was to take a hard look at what was and what wasn't in an everyday layer cake as compared to a Carvel cake.

For example, as shocking as it might seem, a slice of cake has more calories, more fat, and more sodium. In addition to having less of the bad stuff, a slice of Carvel cake has more calcium, more Vitamin A, and more Vitamin B.

Less bad stuff and more good stuff is what parents sure do like to give to their kids.

But whatever strategy they choose, how well they do in taking on this new competition will, in great measure, determine how well the repositioned Carvel will do in the future.

THE LESSON

When the market changes, many times the new direction that should be taken is right in front of your eyes. Yet it remains unseen. That's because often it's viewed as being part of your business when in reality it's more than that, it's your future business. Instead of looking for something new, start with what you may be taking for granted. The obvious answer for Carvel: Let them eat cake!

TEN

Repositioning an Accounting Firm

E ven the staid, conservative world of accounting firms hasn't been immune to change.

For many years, "The Big Eight" quietly did their work and charged their fees. It was said they all belonged to a stuffy men's club, from which real competition was banned.

Then one day, the United States was no longer the center of the economic universe. Continental Europe and Asia had become strong players in what had become the global economy.

Suddenly, all of The Big Eight's clients faced increased competition, which only led them to a drive for more competitiveness and lower fees. This spelled the need for change in client service industries, where anticipating change had never been a hallmark.

The First "Megamerger"

Sensing all this, Larry Horner, then chairman of the U.S. firm of KPMG Peat Marwick, decided that what was needed was an international network of firms to serve this new world order.

So he spent about six years racking up gargantuan frequent-flyer mileage. When the dust settled, he had put together a network called KPMG which now totals 1100 offices in 837 cities in 134 countries.

Exhausted and fed up with airline food, he then turned

over the baton to Jon Madonna, whose job it was to figure out what to *do* with all this.

As Jon said: "I knew we just couldn't sit by the phone and wait for business. We had to develop some new services as well as a new position, to carry us into the next century."

Jon needed some repositioning.

What Was in the Mind?

When we started on this project it wasn't hard to figure out what the problem was in the prospect's mind.

"The Big Six," that's what. KPMG Peat Marwick's marketing problem was the fact that the firm was lumped together with five other accounting firms. (It used to be The Big Eight, before several firms merged.)

Even worse, industry research showed that KPMG was not at the top of the pack. When you looked at the published ratings by prospects, KPMG was in what we call "the mushy middle." (These were compiled by *The Bowman Report,* a newsletter that polls corporate financial executives.)

> Arthur Andersen.....................................7.2
>
> Price Waterhouse................................. 6.9
>
> Ernst & Young...6.5
>
> KPMG Peat Marwick............................6.4
>
> Coopers & Lybrand...............................6.4
>
> Deloitte & Touche................................ 6.2

While The Big Six firms were all created equal, it appeared that some were now more equal than others. If the accounting field has a leader, that leader would be Arthur Andersen, as they are perceived as being the largest in the United States.

The only other firm to have built a mental position for itself is Price Waterhouse. They are known by financial executives as the "blue chip" firm, because they audit a number of America's biggest companies. Of course, the public knows them better as the Academy Awards firm, the one that tabulates the votes. (The envelope, please...)

To counter their low awareness and ratings, some of the other firms are beginning to run expensive advertising programs.

Coopers & Lybrand, for example, have spent several millions on the Super Bowl, plugging the theme: "Not just knowledge. Know-how." What's the difference between knowledge and know-how? Not much.

Deloitte & Touche runs advertisements with the theme "We listen. We deliver." Sounds like a great tagline for Domino's Pizza.

Those are all *slogans*, not differentiating ideas.

A Different Perspective

We decided to look at the competitive situation another way. One that introduced what we call "shifting the battlefield" to an area where KPMG has an advantage.

In the mind of the prospect, KPMG Peat Marwick is buried in third place, after Arthur Andersen and Price Waterhouse.

We were able to point to a parallel marketing situation, to show how a shifting-the-battlefield strategy could work.

It's the air cargo business, which has been dominated by the domestic carriers Federal Express and United Parcel.

Then DHL arrived on the scene. They didn't say that DHL is better than Federal Express and United Parcel. They said, "We are expert in worldwide air cargo services, and our competitors are not."

KPMG is in exactly the same position that DHL was. They may not be the leader domestically, but they're the world's largest accounting firm. That may surprise you. It did us, when we discovered buried in their material this list of the 1992 worldwide revenues of The Big Six accounting firms:

KPMG Peat Marwick..................$6.2 billion

Ernst & Young..............................5.7 billion

Arthur Andersen...........................5.6 billion

Coopers & Lybrand........................5.3 billion

Deloitte & Touche.........................4.8 billion

Price Waterhouse..........................3.8 billion

The Global Leader

Actually, they have always recognized their strength on the worldwide scene, they just hadn't verbalized it.

In fact, in their "statement of credentials" they use the globe as their visual. And their external house magazine is called *The World,* of course.

So the obvious repositioning strategy was to move them out of The Big Six and make them "the global leader."

Their leadership had not one but two dimensions. They had leadership in global size, and leadership in global services.

Interestingly, the global leader position also took care of the perceptual problem of why KPMG isn't the U.S. leader. ("How come Andersen is bigger in the United States? Because our business is more global.")

In addition, it gives prospects a simple factual reason (global experience) for switching from a U.S. to a global accounting firm.

This reason is a powerful weapon, because business itself is becoming more and more global.

Take exports, for example. A January 18, 1993, front-page headline in *The Wall Street Journal* read: MANY U.S. COMPANIES EXPECT STRONG EXPORTS, DESPITE TALK OF SLUMP. The story went on:

Exports matter more to the U.S. than ever before. Over the past six years, merchandise exports have doubled, to nearly $450 billion last year, and now represent some 20 percent of the U.S. industrial output.

We suspected that KPMG could take advantage of the global business trend by running ads with the headline:

> "If your business is global,
> you need a global accounting firm."

New Services

This strategy also set up a need to offer new services to companies entering the global economy. Things like: Benchmarking, Privatization, International Taxes, ISO-9000 Certification, and Transfer Pricing.

Just announcing your new position is never enough. You have to bring it to life with new products and services.

When you make a leadership claim, people tend to subconsciously say "Prove it!" The list of global revenues certainly was one form of proof. But following that with new and interesting global services would reinforce those perceptions, and add further validity to the concept of "Global Leader."

Selling to 6000 Partners

Repositioning a partnership is about as tough as it gets. There are a lot of folks who feel they have a vote.

Recognizing this, Jon Madonna set up a series of road shows to carry his message across the country. As he saw it, the internal sell would be more difficult than the external sell. "My major challenge," reported Jon, "was to change the mindset of partners doing the same things for 20 or 30 years."

A public relations program was focused on positioning Jon

Madonna as a spokesman on global business issues. He was featured as such in op-ed pieces and interviews with both general-news and business media and the accounting trade press.

A series of regular, internal memoranda about the new program was sent to partners and employees.

The firm's quarterly video news-magazine program, called *Insight*, featured examples of how people in the firm were living role models of the global leadership concept. The firm's all-personnel, monthly newspaper also carried stories supporting the repositioning.

Communication tools were developed to equip people with the information they needed on The Global Leader message. It included a question-and-answer sheet to help them deal with those questions that clients might raise.

The annual meeting of partners in the United States, in the fall of 1993, featured The Global Leader theme. The theme was carried out through presentations on the impact of the global economy on business (Robert Reich) and on government (Vernon Jordan), and through a panel discussion on the internationalizing of thinking that featured several U.S. and international KPMG partners. Buttons also carried the theme, and banners with "proof points" of global leadership were strung throughout the Marriott World Center in Orlando.

A Global Business Magazine

Last, but not least, the firm launched a global business magazine called *Worldbusiness*. It was aimed at the five most senior management members in corporations and academia, as well as at high-level government office holders (city, state, federal, and international).

The goal is to use the magazine as a relationship marketing tool, leveraging the firm's status as The Global Leader in business advisory services. It is the only publication of its kind that focuses exclusively on global business (no war, famine, politics), and is also unique in its audience reach: more than 150,000 of the world's most senior members of organizational management. Together with internal distributions throughout the KPMG network, and 20,000 or so used for direct-mail programs, the total circulation is now 200,000. They hope to push that number closer to 300,000 in 1995.

THE LESSON

The lesson here is that sometimes you have to put enormous energy into inside selling before you can get to the outside selling. While partnerships are unique animals, *any* company in the process of repositioning itself should figure on a major internal program to get everyone pointed in the same direction.

In the case of KPMG Peat Marwick, it was a lesson well learned and well executed.

Repositioning Political Candidates

All politics is perception, posturing, and positioning.

Political spin doctors are becoming positioning mavens. They have to, or they won't survive. Given the endless polling that goes on in politics, no other business spends as much money and time crawling around in people's minds.

All this really began to intensify in the late '80s. In fact, the 1988 Bush/Dukakis battle may have been the first presidential election to be decided by the power of the nominee's advertising. But it sure won't be the last.

Anthony Lewis, a columnist for *The New York Times*, said, "It was ungenerous of Mr. Bush in his victory speech to give credit to many but not to his ad man, Roger Ailes."

In the future, the battle for the presidency will become a battle of storyboards. It will also become a battle of negative commercials. The 1988 Boston Harbor and Willy Horton commercials of the Bush campaign are destined to go down in political history, along with the 1964 anti-Goldwater "daisy" commercial of Lyndon Johnson. (For you young readers, this commercial repositioned Mr. Goldwater as a trigger-happy cold-war warrior who might blow up the world.)

Repositioning Your Competition

1988 also was a difficult year for Lowell Weicker, a U.S. senator from the state of Connecticut. He was seeking reelection to a fourth term. His Democratic opponent, Connecticut Attorney General Joe Lieberman, faced what most political pundits described as a hopeless uphill fight. What ensued was not only surprising, but a textbook example of repositioning.

Throughout Lowell Weicker's senate career, he was known as a political maverick, fiercely independent in outlook and demeanor. He was always the politician willing to challenge the most powerful, regardless of the personal consequences. He took on the Nixon administration in the Watergate hearings. He challenged Ronald Reagan's policies. He even took on Jesse Helms.

His campaign slogan, "Nobody's man but yours," had positioned him as a maverick in every campaign from 1976 to 1988. He loved a good fight. (At 6' 7", it's no wonder.)

Enter Joe Lieberman, in the spring of 1988. Facing daunting odds, Lieberman shrewdly constructed an advertising campaign to reposition Weicker as a man out-of-touch with mainstream Connecticut. A man selfishly using his office to advance causes of little importance to anyone but Weicker.

He cited the example of honorariums that Weicker had received at distant locations, while important business was being ignored in Washington. He talked about Weicker positions on matters that didn't seem important to Connecticut voters, such as diplomatic relations with Cuba.

Lieberman cleverly took "Nobody's man but yours" and repositioned Weicker as self-interested and self-promoting—in effect, as "Nobody's man but Lowell's." Put simply, Lieberman struck at a weakness in the Weicker perception of "maverick," using it to sustain claims of political arrogance and distance.

Lowell Weicker lost in a very close election. (10,000 votes.)

Repositioning Yourself

Defeat, however, did not end Lowell Weicker's political career. In March of 1990, with the help of Tom D'Amore and "positioning maven" Peter Gold, Weicker launched a campaign for the governorship of Connecticut. In this historic race, Weicker successfully repositioned himself from Republican to Independent, taking advantage of the maverick position he had owned in voters' minds for decades.

Using the symbolism of a new political party called the Connecticut Party, as well as powerful rhetoric attacking entrenched party politics, Weicker succeeded in repositioning himself. The result was that he gained election as Connecticut's first independent Governor. Something that hadn't been done in 136 years.

In 1992, George Bush failed to reposition himself. Instead, he stood pat while the electorate's attitudes shifted. America wanted change and an end to gridlock. Americans also weren't very happy with the economy.

Clinton had positioned himself as a new-generation leader who could change things in Washington.

Repositioning George Bush

How should Mr. Bush have repositioned himself? Always start with perceptions.

First, he should have started with the positive perception the public would have accorded him, that of "world leader." Foreign policy also happened to be Mr. Clinton's biggest weakness. (Being Governor of Arkansas doesn't give you much international experience.)

Then, Mr. Bush had to dramatize the importance of what was going on in the world, and how it would impact the economy and jobs at home. With the end of the Cold War, the global economy had become the new game in town. New countries were emerging as *industrial powers* almost on a monthly basis. (Winning markets does more for a country than winning wars. If you doubt this, just check out Japan.)

It would take a person with wide international experience

and powerful personal relationships with other world leaders to help steer the United States through those troubled economic waters.

But all of that still wasn't enough.

Promoting a New and Improved Presidency

As we say in marketing, President Bush & Co. had to do something to the product to get people's attention. What was called for was a "new and improved" strategy. One that signaled change.

His natural move would have been to take his best asset, James Baker, and add him to the product. In other words, make him the Vice President. (That would have dealt with the inept Quayle problem.)

But that *still* wouldn't have been enough, as the V.P. job is widely perceived as a do-nothing job.

What the President had to do was restructure the job description of the V.P. He should have made him his "Chief Operating Officer" in charge of domestic policy. This was where the public was focused, and Mr. Baker's enormous experience as Reagan's Chief of Staff, Secretary of the Treasury, and Secretary of State made him highly qualified to help structure a domestic policy that would focus on making America more competitive on the global scene. (Quite simply, a country that generates jobs.)

Of course, Mr. Bush would continue to work closely with Mr. Baker on both international and domestic problems. (CEOs always work closely with their COOs.)

The message: Two experienced world leaders are in a far better position to deal with these turbulent times, both internationally and domestically. What do you want, real experience or *The Gong Show?* (This also would have repositioned Mr. Clinton as "inexperienced.")

By *not* repositioning himself, George Bush paid the price

of not being elected. He lost sight of change.

Repositioning Yourself, Inadvertently

One of the things politicians do quite often is reposition themselves *by mistake*. Usually by putting their foot in their mouth.

Nobody's mouth has gotten him into political trouble as quickly as Ross Perot's.

When he was positioned as a folksy "gadfly," haranguing those inept bureaucrats in Washington, he sounded fine. But when he tried to reposition himself as a candidate of presidential timbre, it was a different story.

First there was the sudden change of plans, when he withdrew from the race because he had heard that some nasty Republicans were going to disrupt his daughter's wedding.

When Americans heard that, most said to themselves, "Why not call the caterer and move the date? This little fellow is beginning to sound paranoid." Doubts about his being a serious candidate began to build. Despite that, when he reentered the race he still got 20 percent of the vote. His infomercials weren't bad, and his money bought a lot of audience.

Then came the big TV debate with Al Gore on NAFTA. Whoops! As we all know, Mr. Gore is no debating giant. He's a nice guy, but he can lull you to sleep. But next to Ross, he sounded like Mario Cuomo.

That was all America had to hear. Mr. Perot is now positioned not as a serious candidate but as a perennial gadfly.

Repositioning Mr. Clinton

Given the Republican resurgence in the 1994 congressional elections, Mr. Clinton must now come up with what *The Washington Post* calls "repositioning plans."

It won't be easy.

For a good many years, the Republican Party has been positioned by the Democrats as the minority party of the rich and the status quo. In fact, the presidential race of 1992 helped to solidify that perception. Patrician George Bush, and his tired brand of GOPers, were outflanked by an aggressive young southern Governor who broke onto the scene as a champion of change and the middle class.

Bill Clinton's problem? He has forgotten who and what made him President. People actually took seriously his promise of change. And when voters began to perceive that he wasn't fixing things, but waffling and being consumed by forces within his hopelessly fragmented party, they rebelled.

Now Newt Gingrich occupies center stage. In the elections of 1994, he led the Republican effort to gain control of the House of Representatives, devising the strategy that was to put them in charge for the first time in 40 years.

In the fall of 1994, Newt, along with 300 candidates for Congress, staged the announcement of a bold political pledge, the "Contract with America." The Contract called for dramatic change in the House as an institution, for tax and spending cuts, and for a return to core societal values.

Republicans Have Been Repositioned

And a funny thing happened on the way to the polls. America took it very seriously. The Republicans have successfully repositioned themselves as the party of the middle class and change (if not "revolution"), and Newt Gingrich and his colleagues are, at least for the time being, in the catbird's seat.

Gingrich's persistence, in the days following the '94 election and in the opening days of the new session of Congress, prove once again that "Pursuit is a second act of victory, in many cases more important than the first." (A quote from Karl von Clausewitz, the philosopher of war and hero of our *Marketing Warfare* book.) Newt's love of the limelight has helped to complete the repositioning of his party with America as a whole. All of us have been made aware of the Contract, through a very concerted and focused communications effort by the new Speaker.

This has all been very impressive. (I wonder if Mr. Gingrich, who is reported to be an avid reader, has read the first book on "Positioning"?)

Time will tell, for now he has to make sure the Republicans get it done. He also has to reposition himself from "loud-mouth" to "leader" if he wants to command an important place in history.

Some Observations on Spin Doctors

There are a great many consultants in the game of politics, and they tend to make two mistakes. First, many of them cut their teeth working for one of the congressional candidates. They enjoy success in a single campaign (in someplace like Tennessee), then go out on their own and apply formulas that worked in one race to all others.

In fact it's those very formulas, used indiscriminately, that have led to an overreliance on attack advertising in campaigns and the resulting credibility crisis facing most politicians. Campaigns are *marketing problems,* and they need to be treated with the same discipline needed to win the cola wars.

Consultants also tend to spend far too much time and money on research and the neurotic analysis of data. Most effective campaigns are built around simple ideas that are not the by-product of research.

For that matter, once elected, most modern-day Presidents appear to continue to be trapped by the poll takers.

Instead of making decisions on what they feel is best for the country, they tend to make decisions on what their advisors tell them will play best in the land of public opinion.

Abraham Lincoln certainly wouldn't have become one of our greatest Presidents if he listened to the polls. He became a giant by making unpopular decisions that he felt were right.

THE LESSON

The infinite variety of cross-tabulations and subsets of data, provided by research, frequently lead political consultants and marketers to pick up false signals from the market-place. Or at a minimum, to overcomplicate the message of a campaign.

Programs that recognize *the power of simplicity and consistency* are the ones that most often succeed.

Repositioning a Television Show

Television can be a difficult business. You get a hot show idea, and before you know it you're surrounded by competitors doing something similar.

Look at all the tabloid shows. Or the talk shows. Or the sitcoms. Very few have a chance to run a successful show for any length of time.

All this makes for an interesting repositioning case study on a show we've all seen called *Entertainment Tonight*. (You know, Mary Hart and John Tesh.)

A Call from the Coast

It all began with the first cellular phone call I ever received from the West Coast. The lady on the telephone was Lucie Salhany, head of Paramount Television. Her problem: declining ratings. My assignment: help find a way to turn them around. I jumped at it. (Hanging around the back lot of a movie studio had to be more fun than hanging around an IBM conference room.)

The show had peaked in 1984. Then came four straight years of declining ratings. This put the syndicated show in jeopardy, because local television stations were beginning to refuse the show the best time slots.

What Perceptions Showed

The first thing I looked at was some of the research they had collected on the show.

When regular viewers were asked if they were disappointed after watching, the research said that 85 percent were "rarely" or "never" disappointed. The show was appreciated and well received.

But a follow-up question asked viewers if they would be disappointed if the show were canceled.

Very revealing. Seventy-one percent said they would be "not very" or only "somewhat" disappointed if *Entertainment Tonight* went away. One reason was probably the fact that a viewer could now get this kind of information from so many other places.

After seven years, *ET* had reached a point where it was taken for granted by many viewers. The show suffered from a bad case of the blahs. This is not good news for a television show. Loyalty is what drives show ratings.

Surrounded by Competition

A quick check of the TV listings readily dramatized the problem. *ET* was surrounded by competition. Where once it had reigned supreme, there were now a dozen or more enemies in the battle for "news of entertainment."

To name a few, the *Today* and *Good Morning, America* shows, especially in their second hours. The entertainment and celebrity coverage on expanded local news shows. Barbara Walters specials, *Lifestyles of the Rich and Famous*. And the new breed of tabloid talk shows that devote a fair amount of time to the entertainment beat. There was also Group W's entertainment report. And a raft of cable offerings: HBO's *Behind the Scenes*, CNN's *Hollywood Minute*, USA Cable's *Hollywood Insider*.

The bottom line was this steadily rising tide of competition, eating away at ratings and undercutting audience loyalty.

This continuous pressure comes to all companies, as markets mature. The trick is to constantly attack *yourself* with new and better ideas. If you don't change, you become an easy target. If you keep moving and improving, the competition can never get a bead on you.

Needed: A New and Improved Show

It was apparent to us that if *ET* couldn't get its competitors to go away, it would have to refocus or reposition away from "news" to something else. But what?

Well, Fats Waller wrote a lyric that gave us our answer: "Find out what they like and how they like it, and let them have it just that way."

Sometimes you don't have to resort to expensive research to find out what people like. A "trick of the trade" that few exploit can be learned by studying the business of a different category that is selling a related product.

Obviously, a number of magazines also were doing "news of entertainment." One of them was *People* magazine. An analysis showed that they had been through an editorial change, and were no longer what they had started out as. (Sort of a less expensive *Life*.)

Just a look at the covers quickly showed us that *People* had lowered its level and was writing far more "inside" stuff and gossip.

Their circulation gains also proved that this is what people want. By giving readers more exposés and juicy stuff, in four years their circulation had increased from 2.7 to around 3.3 million readers.

They weren't alone. *People, Us, The Star,* and *National Enquirer* were also feeding Americans the behind-the-scenes, gossipy stuff they truly love. The combined circulation of these four was also up significantly. In total, the weekly readership of these magazines was 56 million gossip-lovers.

All those inquiring minds were wondering, "Who's doing what to whom?" That was the market *ET* had to tap. (As far as I can tell, there's simply no bottom to America's lust for this kind of material. People can't get enough.)

The Shift from "News" to "Inside"

Based on this study, our recommendation was to shift the show's focus to much more "inside" information. That's "what they like," so give it to them "just that way." Create a show that people can't stand to miss.

Also, "inside" is much more than gossip. If you look at a dictionary definition it means: "things known only to insiders; the inside story; going inside a situation; going behind the scenes."

But to make this work, *ET* had to reinforce the "inside" concept by retitling show segments and reports to give them an "inside" feeling. ("Inside Movies," "Inside Television," "Inside Rock & Roll," etc.)

Another need was aggressive "Coming Attractions" promotion. During the time the show was going "inside," they had to find a way to build awareness for this shift in focus. That meant doing a lot of "Coming Attractions" they could feed to their stations, so they could promote the upcoming shows. The juicier the promo, the better.

A Happy Ending

Entertainment Tonight went from "news" to "inside," and it did so exceptionally well. One major reason for the successful implementation was Lucie Salhany. Once she felt that this was the proper way to reposition the show, she made sure it happened and happened right. Her role was critical. (In the last chapter we tell you why.)

There's a happy ending to this repositioning story. The slide was stopped, and the show's ratings climbed back up toward their earlier highs.

Hollywood itself couldn't have written a better plot.

THE LESSON

There are times when you have to change your product, as a way of escaping from competitive pressures. When sitting there and slugging it out just isn't productive.

What you're after is a "new and improved" version that enables you to rise above your competition.

Although in the *ET* case, I suppose it was a move to "get below" their competition.

Repositioning an Oil Company

*P*rivatization has become a big buzzword in the global economy. And going from "government-owned" to "privately owned" calls for—you guessed it—repositioning.

Such was the case when Spain's national oil company privatized. When the government was in charge, it was all the National Institute of Hydrocarbons. Then a new company called Repsol was formed, and in 1989, stock was sold to the public.

When the dust settled, the new company had three of the country's gasoline brands and about half of its gas stations. There was a new brand created when the company went private (Repsol). Then there was the old, well-known brand of government-owned days (Campsa). Finally, there was a regional brand in the north of Spain (Petronor).

All this would be like one U.S. oil company owning Mobil, Texaco, and Arco. (Not a bad deal, if you could get away with it.)

Now you might say, what's the marketing problem with an arrangement like that? Well, the question we were asked to answer was, "What should be done with these brands?"

It seems that the new organization was treating them all the same. It was as if they had one brand inside the company and three brands outside. Something deep down inside told Oscar Fanjul, the Chairman, that there should be a better way to go to market with these brands.

The Multi-Brand Approach

There *is* a better way.

While you can save marketing money by sticking with one brand, experience has shown that multiple brands can translate to bigger overall market share. Nike and Levi's, big single brands, each has about 30 percent of its respective market.

Gillette, on the other hand, has four brands (Trac II, Atra, Sensor, Good News) and has 65 percent of its market. We call this "the complementary approach," as you have brands that complement rather than compete with one another.

This calls for different names, different positions, and different target audiences.

Repsol had the different names, but that was it. What was needed was a repositioning strategy that would add different strategies aimed at different market segments. As we combed through their research, it became apparent that there were some obvious strategies for them to pursue.

A Brand for the Car

Thanks to a great deal of corporate introductory advertising about the new Repsol brand, most people in Spain gave this new company high marks in "innovation and technology." Also, the Repsol brand had pioneered 98-octane gasoline. (Something even the United States doesn't have.) All this tended to set up a strategy that would focus on people that were very car-oriented. And since cars are very expensive in Spain, this was a large percentage of people.

The concept that captured this strategy was

"Repsol. The best for your car."

Of course, to bring this concept to life they had to focus on car-oriented products and promotion. In addition to 98-octane gasoline, we recommended that they develop a new synthetic oil called "Multi-valve" for today's new engines.

Also, that they should consider an auto-products focus in their station stores. And continue the Repsol racing program. Everything should have a car focus, especially their advertising.

A Brand for Service

Perceptual research showed that the long-term Campsa brand was perceived very favorably. In terms of "reliability," it scored exceptionally high as compared to other gas-station brands. (Even 50 percent higher than the new Repsol brand.)

This led us to recommend that Campsa should take advantage of these perceptions and emphasize its many years of service to the Spanish motorist. The way to express this idea:

"Campsa. Sixty years of service."

The way to implement this strategy was to continue to publish their very popular *Campsa Driving Guide.* (Maps, restaurants, hotels, etc.)

Campsa stations also had begun to put 7-Eleven stores in certain locations. We recommended that they extend these stores to all locations, as well as introduce any new service ideas they had on the drawing board. A typical example of this would be the credit card self-service pumps you see at many stations in the United States.

It turned out that Campsa also was sponsoring a racing program. In this case we recommended that they discontinue the program and leave the racing to Repsol.

Of course the Campsa advertising could take viewers through the 60 years of service, thus reminding people of the excellent job they have done for six decades.

Interestingly, the heating-oil brand also was that of Campsa. The company was in the process of introducing a three-hour emergency-delivery program. What better idea to dramatize their commitment to "service"?

A Brand for Price

The last brand was regional, and really had no strong perceptions attached to it. In effect it had a clean slate in the mind,
and could be repositioned in any way one wanted.

We saw a future possibility for Petronor as a price brand.
The way to express this concept:

"Petronor. More miles for your money."

In terms of explanation, this brand would be put in high-
volume locations, have self-service pumps only, have low
prices, limited services, and be paid for in cash only.

While price is not yet an issue in Spanish gasoline, this
brand certainly could be set up if price wars ever do break out.

Multiple Positions

These three brands now had three different positions. Repsol:
car; Campsa: *service*; Petronor: *price*.

Of course, there were product implications for this complementary approach.

New car-technology products should be launched and
advertised only by Repsol. New service products should be
launched and advertised only by Campsa. As for organizational
implications, each brand should have its own sales and marketing departments. These should compete with each other,
and support functions should be non-branded.

Research and new-product development should be corporate functions.

A top management committee should oversee brand differ-
entiation, as well as resource allocation. This is a critical step
in the process. Unless senior management stays involved, mul-
tiple-brand strategies often lose focus as middle-level brand
managers seek growth by chasing all parts of the market.
(That's what caused the GM problem.)

More on this is presented in Chapter 21 which talks about the need of having the right people in the room when important strategic decisions are being made.

THE LESSON

Sometimes you have to change things today, so that you're ready for tomorrow.

All this repositioning work has set up Repsol to better handle the arrival of the multinational oil companies in Spain. Shell, Mobil, and BP will not have as much maneuvering room, as Repsol now has the three major segments covered.

As we figure it, the big oil company in Spain should stay the big oil company in Spain—thanks to a little repositioning.

PART THREE

The Tricks
of the Trade

For things we have to learn before we can do them, we learn by doing them.

ARISTOTLE

CHAPTER FOURTEEN

Minds Work
by Ear

Has anyone ever asked you which is more powerful, the eye or the ear? Probably not, because the answer is obvious. I'll bet that deep down inside, you believe the eye is more powerful than the ear. Call it "visual chauvinism," if you like, but it's a preconception held by many marketing people.

I'll bet, too, that you share a related preconception, first expressed some 500 years before the birth of Christ. Confucius says: "A picture is worth a thousand words."

Those seven words—not *pictures*, mind you, but *words*—have lived for 2500 years. And the way things have been going lately, it seems like those seven words will never die.

What agency president, creative director, or art director hasn't quoted Confucius at least once in his or her career?

What Positioning Taught Us

After analyzing hundreds of effective positioning programs, we ran into a surprising conclusion:

The programs were all verbal. There wasn't a single positioning concept that was exclusively visual. Could Confucius have been wrong?

We have come to the conclusion that the mind works by ear, not by eye.

A picture is *not* worth a thousand words.

If you looked just at the pictures in almost any magazine or newspaper, you would earn very little. If you read just the words, however, you would have a pretty good idea of what was what.

In spite of the evidence all around us, communications people suffer from wordophobia, a morbid fear of words. In order to set the record straight, we went back to find out exactly what it was Confucius had said. We took the Chinese characters and had them translated.

Confucius said: "A picture is worth a thousand pieces of gold." Not *words*, but *gold*!

We knew instantly that here was a true prophet. What Confucius foresaw was television and the movies, where a picture does indeed sell for thousands of pieces of gold. Son of a gun! And here, all these years, I thought he was knocking *words*!

What Is a Picture Worth?

We all know that television pictures are expensive. Just 30 seconds' worth of pictures during Super Bowl XXIX would have set you back $1.2 million.

But what is a *picture* worth on television? That is, *just* the picture, without the sound?

Not much. As a matter of fact, without the words on the package or the graphics on the screen, pictures in a TV commercial have almost no communication value. But add sound, and the "picture" changes.

If pictures alone make no sense, how about sound alone? Strange as it may seem, the sound alone in a television commercial usually carries an easy-to-understand message.

Most classic print advertisements illustrate the same principle. The visual alone makes almost no sense.

Naturally, a print ad with *both* pictures and words is more effective than either the words or the pictures alone. But which is more powerful individually, the verbal or the visual?

Sound Alone Is Powerful

Take the classic "Pepsi-Cola hits the spot" radio commercial, which first ran 56 years ago.

Nothing, absolutely nothing, went into the mind via the eye. Yet the commercial hit a hot spot. Even today some people can recall the opening bits of Pepsi music, and are then able to recite every word of the jingle. Fifty-six years later!

That's interesting. An idea deeply embedded in the mind that didn't come in through the eyes. Something seems wrong with the conventional wisdom as to the superiority of the eye.

In order to obtain a more objective viewpoint on the subject, we went out and found an expert, the author of the authoritative book on the subject of memory. Dr. Elizabeth Loftus of the University of Washington is a psychologist, teacher, researcher, and author of more than 8 books and 100 articles on the human mind and how it works. When we asked her which is superior, the eye or the ear, this was her reply:

> In many ways the ear is superior to the eye. What I mean by that is that there is evidence from controlled laboratory studies that shows that when you present a list of words to people, and you present it either auditorily, say on a tape recorder, or you present it visually, say on slides, people remember more words if they hear the words than if they see them.

Words Are Powerful

> In order to understand *why*, you have to realize that there are essentially two kinds of memory. There is iconic memory, which stores visual images, and echoic memory, which stores auditory images. When the eye sees some picture or takes in some visual information, a fairly complete image registers itself in iconic memory, but it fades away fairly quickly, on the order of say a second or so. However, when the ear takes in information, it too registers a fairly complete

image, but it fades away more slowly, say on the order of four to five seconds.

So as you can see, the echoic memory for auditory information lasts longer than the iconic memory for visual information.

What about pictures? Is a picture worth a thousand words? Dr. Loftus responded:

> I don't think that is really true. You know, you hear that sticks and stones can break my bones but words will never hurt me. It is just not true; words can really hurt you very, very much. Sometimes words can help you, and words can be powerful.
>
> In fact, the power of the spoken word never really stops. There is an important study that shows that even people who are anesthetized during surgery, if they are hypnotized later, can remember some of the things that were spoken, some of the sounds they heard during the surgery.

Of course, that happens when people are asleep, or close to it. We run ads when people are awake. What about under those more normal circumstances? Dr. Loftus again:

> A study from Northwestern University shows that if you try to convince people about a product—it happened to be a shampoo—and you do it with just a verbal message, people are much more persuaded about your product. They like it better, they want to buy it more than if you accompany these verbal messages with pictures. The verbal message alone seems to create in people's minds more of a positive feeling for the product.

Two Kinds of Words

To summarize, there are two kinds of words: printed and spoken. We often confuse the two, but there's a big difference.

The ear is faster than the eye. Repeated tests have shown

that the mind is able to understand a spoken word in 140 milliseconds. A printed word, on the other hand, is able to be understood in 180 milliseconds.

To account for this 40-millisecond delay, psychologists speculate that the brain translates visual information into aural sounds that the mind can comprehend.

Not only do you hear faster than you see, your hearing lasts longer than your seeing. A visual image, whether picture or words, fades away in one second, unless your mind does something to file away the essence of the idea. Hearing, on the other hand, lasts four or five times as long.

That's why it's easy to lose your train of thought when you're reading printed words. Often you have to backtrack, to pick up the sense of the message. Because sound lasts much longer in the mind, the spoken word is easier to follow.

Listening to a message is much more effective than reading it. Two things are different. First, the mind holds the spoken words in storage much longer, enabling you to follow the train of thought with greater clarity. And second, the tone of the human voice gives the words an emotional impact that the printed words alone cannot impart.

But there are other things that happen in your mind when you listen to the spoken word.

Tone of Voice

What about the contribution that tone of voice adds to communication? We turned to another expert, Thomas Sticht, psychologist, researcher, and author of 5 books and 95 articles on communication. He replied:

> We conducted research for the United States Army in which we presented a speech without any tone to it, and found that comprehension and learning were very poor. When we added natural inflection and intonation, then comprehension and learning were greatly improved.

So the tone, the rhythm that we add to the spoken language, which is not in the written language really does help in the learning process.

The Mind Works by Ear

And of course, we couldn't resist asking Mr. Sticht whether a picture is indeed worth a thousand words. His response:

> I'd like to think that one word is worth a thousand pictures. As a matter of fact, how many times have you seen pictures trying to represent concepts? Words such as God, trustworthiness, reliability, and love. It is very hard to represent those concepts in pictures, and so I'd like to think that in many cases one word is worth a thousand pictures.

The relationship between the two kinds of words may be of interest to you. We have found that written language is recoded by the mind into an internal form of oral language. It seems that your mind must translate printed words into their spoken equivalents before it can understand them. (The beginning reader moves his or her lips when reading.)

The ear drives the eye. There is much evidence that the mind works by ear. That thinking is a process of manipulating *sounds*, not images. (Even when pictures or photographs are involved.) As a result, you *see* what you *hear*, what the sound has led you to *expect* to see, not what the eye tells you it *has* seen.

Beauty Is Only Name-Deep

A classic experiment has demonstrated this point. The experimenter identified two women whom a group of people had rated as being equal in beauty.

Then he went to a second group and added the dimension of sound. He added *names*. One woman was given the name

Jennifer, the other Gertrude. What do you think happened when this second group voted on which woman was the prettier?

You got it. The results were 158 votes for Jennifer, 39 votes for Gertrude. Our apologies to all you Gertrudes out there, but you see the problem. "Gertrude" is simply an unpleasant sound that distorts people's view of things.

The Power of a Sound Name

In *Positioning: The Battle for Your Mind*, we said: "The name is the hook that hangs the brand on the product ladder in the prospect's mind."

Now we know *why*. Apparently, thinking itself involves the manipulation of sounds deep inside the brain. Even when the stimulus is purely visual, as with printed words.

Shakespeare was wrong: A rose by any other name would *not* smell as sweet! Not only do you see what you want to see, you also smell what you want to smell. Which is why the single most important decision in the marketing of a perfume is the name you decide to put on the brand.

Would "Alfred" perfume have sold as well as "Charlie"? We doubt it. And Hog Island in the Caribbean was going nowhere until its name was changed to Paradise Island. (For more on the power of a good sounding name, see Chapter 15.)

"Language and writing," said Ferdinand de Saussure, a famous Belgian linguist, "are two distinct systems of signs. The second exists for the sole purpose of representing the first." Translation: Print is a secondary medium that exists as a representation of the primary medium of sound.

Implications for Advertising

The implications of these findings for the advertising industry are staggering. In many ways, they call for a complete reorientation from the visual to the verbal point of view.

This isn't to say that the visual doesn't play an important role. Of course it does. But the verbal should be the driver, while the pictures reinforce the words. All too often the opposite is the case.

First off, then, the printed words should carry the bulk of the sales message. Cutesy or confusing words bring nothing but trouble.

Second, headlines should *sound* good, as well as look good. The rhyme or rhythm of the words can be powerful memory devices.

Finally, pictures need a very quick explanation, as otherwise they will distract readers. "Stopping" people won't accomplish much, if they *look* but don't *read*.

In a television commercial, spoken words should carry the sales message. Most important, you should never let the pictures and movements overwhelm the sound. When this happens, viewers stop listening and little communication takes place.

This "distraction factor" explains why so many commercials tend to be misidentified by the public. It also explains why Procter & Gamble's much-maligned slice-of-life approach works so well. The format is verbally driven, and rarely contains any visual distractions. People don't rave about their commercials, they just *remember* them.

The Consumer Prefers the Ear

When people communicate with one another, the ear is the preferred avenue of entry, either in person (word of mouth) or over the phone.

There are many ways to prove that the consumer prefers to send and receive information by ear rather than by eye. In 1993, Americans made 522 billion telephone calls and sent 92 billion first-class letters. That's six phone calls for every letter.

But even that isn't the whole story. As every homeowner knows, "first-class mail" usually means nothing but bills. We estimate that the average person makes 20 phone calls for every letter he or she writes.

When people turn to one of the senses for pure pleasure, the sense they generally turn to is the ear. Compare, for example, the time spent listening to music with the time spent looking at art or photography. There's no comparison. The ear wins by a wide margin.

The Advertiser Prefers the Eye

Clearly, there is a striking inconsistency between advertisers and the target of their advertising, the prospects.

Prospects spend 85 percent of their overall media time immersed in ear-oriented media such as radio and television, and only 15 percent of their time with eye-oriented media such as newspapers and magazines.

Advertisers, on the other hand, spend 55 percent of their dollars on eye media (print), and only 45 percent of their dollars on ear media (broadcast).

Is it fair to call television an ear-oriented medium?

Probably not. But research suggests that sound plays a far more important role in the communication effectiveness of television than most advertisers or their agencies are willing to admit.

A final thought about our friend Confucius. We all remember what he *said*, not what he looked like; because minds do work by ear. But as we pointed out in Chapter 3, "minds are confused," and it's a pity we didn't hear him *right!*

Because the mind works by ear.

Secrets to Finding a Good Name

Fifteen years ago, we wrote: "The single most important marketing decision you can make is what to name the product."

By now, the world seems to agree.

A booklet from Johnson & Johnson says: "Our company's name and trademarks are by far our most valuable assets."

The former chairman of Quaker Oats says: "If this business were to be split up, I would be glad to take the brands, trademarks, and goodwill, and you could have all the bricks and mortar—and I would fare better than you."

A former Commissioner of the Patent and Trademark Office said that a trademark is "frequently a more valuable asset of a business than all other assets combined."

A survey of 400 companies shows that, compared to three years ago, marketers are introducing more names, trying more ways to nail down a name, and finding it more difficult to get the job done.

Problem #1: Availability

The availability of names is today's number-one problem. Communications overload is strangling the world of names, too.

There are about 1.6 million registered trademarks in the United States. In just one field—cosmetics—there are 72,100 registered trademarks. And every four months another 1000 cosmetics names are added. (That's eight new trademarks every day of the week. In just one field. In just one country.)

In Europe, there are about 3 million trademarks. Last year more than 500,000 new names were registered around the world.

A standard dictionary has about 100,000 entries. We're running out of words to use for names.

Nine Out of Ten Ideas Won't Make the Cut

So, how hard is it to come up with a good name for a product? Here's how hard. A few years ago, the industrial products sector of Kimberly-Clark actually trademarked the name "Brand X."

How hard is to to name your company? A Nasdaq company CEO ran an employee contest to rename the corporation. It dumped 3400 suggestions into his lap. Not a winner among them.

That's not unusual. Nine of every 10 names you search won't be available.

Let's say you're trying to name a simple product, like a new household glue. You size up the adhesive technology from R&D, you size up the competition, you gather some creative types, and brainstorm a list of possibilities:

Benchmark, Bulldog, First Choice, Grand Slam, Intac, Laser Bond, Laser Loc, Powerhouse, Python, Rock Solid, Samson, Strong Arm, Terminator, Top Grip, Xtra.

Pretty good, huh? Just one small problem. Every one of those names is already taken, already registered by someone else.

Initials Still Aren't Names

AIB   BZW   EG&G   DSC   EMC   SCI   UBS
All-initial names aren't really names at all. From a positioning

standpoint, they're a one-way ticket to oblivion: the "no-name trap," as we call it in *Positioning: The Battle for Your Mind.*

Introduce yourself to someone as "B.J." and your new friend's mind immediately starts trying to translate the initials back into something meaningful. ("I wonder if that's short for Bobbie Joe. Maybe it's Billie Jack. Or...") Meanwhile, old B.J. is chatting away, and no real communication is taking place.

It's the same with company and product names. "Good morning, I'm from HSBC Holdings, and I'd like to—" Hold on there! Holding *who*? You're holding *what*?

HSBC? "It doesn't stand for anything," says Albert Maasland, of the London-based bond and money-market operation named HSBC Holdings PLC. (Great. We're so proud of our firm: Its name doesn't stand for anything!)

Try this simple test. Below are "pairs" of company names taken right out of the *Fortune* 500 listings. Some of the biggest industrial corporations in America, from the most famous business list around. These are names you're going to recognize, right?

The "pairs" are two company names, side by side in the *Fortune* tables. Just one ranking apart. So which half of each pair is better known? Which would you rather have in your portfolio? (Be honest.)

Bethlehem Steel, or VF?

Hershey Foods, or AMP?

Dow Jones, or USG?

Maxus Energy, or EMC?

Interlake, or NCH?

Names that use real or even invented words are about 40 percent easier to remember than alphabet-soup names. Now, alphabet soup may be nourishing stuff, but it's a lousy way to name yourself. (Unless you're hiding from somebody, because a no-name name is the corporate equivalent of a disguise.)

With one exception. Internally, the shorthand abbreviation of a long name into initials makes sense. It's quicker for everyone. So inside the InterMetro Industries Corp. shop, when you say, "Let's pull the whole IMIC team together on this one," presumably everyone understands.

Even so, think ahead. Southern Baptist Hospital merged with Mercy Hospital in New Orleans. A debate developed over whether Mercy or Baptist should come first in the new, combined name. Hope they thought about their internal shorthand. Would you rather be called BM or MB?

The Latest Thinking

Three-quarters of all companies say it's now "significantly more difficult" to come up with a new name, compared to five years ago.

Over the years, we've worked with hundreds of companies as they've searched for the right name. A name that can slice into the mind. A name that can begin the positioning process.

Here's the latest thinking on what to call your baby.

Start the Communications Process

The best names are locked directly to a product benefit or a selling proposition. When you pair the name and the need, the positioning process is off and running every time someone hears or reads or speaks your name.

Over time, your name and the position become almost synonymous. You can own a category in the mind.

DieHard, a long-lasting, tenacious battery. (A word taken right out of the dictionary, long before the movie of the same name starring Bruce Willis.)

L'Eggs for hosiery. Windex for window cleaning. Intensive Care skin lotion. Head & Shoulders shampoo.

You think every possible word is already being used in your category? Keep looking. Go beyond the synonyms into the colloquial, into slang. The Whole Enchilada, for a Mexican restaurant chain. No Sweat, a successful new sports deodorant from Revlon.

Make Sure Your Name Is Pleasing to the Ear

And not just to the eye.

As we saw in Chapter 14, the mind translates words into sounds. Chances are, your name will be said aloud more often than it's read.

Caress is as silky soft as the bath soap itself.

NutraSweet is sweet to the ear. Plus, it's locked to the core idea, and therefore easy to remember.

UNUM, a big insurance company, is harsh to the ear, and ugly off the lips. (Is that "YOU-numb" or "OOO-numb"? Even their receptionists aren't sure.) Beware of names that sound like grunts. By comparison, their previous name—Union Mutual—was a gem.

A 1994 movie called *The Shawshank Redemption* was praised by the critics as an uplifting prison drama. It got several Academy Award nominations. It starred Tim Robbins and Morgan Freeman. And it was saddled with an awful name. The movie cost $27 million but it grossed only $18 million.

The president of Castle Rock Pictures jumps to its defense by pointing out that *The Shawshank Redemption* tested higher in screenings than big hits like *A Few Good Men, When Harry Met Sally,* and *In the Line of Fire.*

Says Castle Rock's Martin Schafer: "We thought it was a good enough movie to overcome the negatives. But we couldn't get audiences in to see it."

Not good enough to overcome a disastrous name. The mind translated those clunky words into ominous sounds. And people got into a different line down at the Tenplex.

Make It Easy to Remember

The repetition of a sound is a powerful aid to memory.

So try to build the themeline at the same time as you're building the name. Here are some stellar examples of coupling the position to the name:

> *Roach Motel.* The roaches check in, but they don't check out.
>
> *Taster's Choice.* Tastes and smells like real ground roast.
>
> *Master Glue.* Masters twice as many materials as ordinary super-glue.
>
> *Fink Used Cars.* Quick as a wink, deal with Fink. [An enormously successful used-car dealer in Zanesville, Ohio.]

Coin a Name with Care

Any nerd with a computer can coin a name like "Anadem" or "Zylog." As a famous theater critic once observed, "That's not writing. That's typing."

Only when you are first in the mind with a truly new product that millions are certain to desire can you afford the luxury of a mean-nothing name.

George Eastman said he coined the name Kodak for a variety of reasons. It was short, unusual, vigorous. "The letter K," he said, "has been a favorite with me—it seemed a strong, incisive sort of letter."

Newly minted words are called *neologisms.* And in a world where trademarks have run amok, and with dictionaries running out of words to exploit, it's obvious you'll often have to go with neologisms.

But as my naming partner, Steve Rivkin, points out, you can coin names that are meaningful, impactful, available—and still start the positioning process.

The corporation name International Multifoods is a crisp word fusion.

Humana, Compaq, and Acura are all altered forms of recognizable words.

So is Trueste, the first new perfume from Tiffany & Co. in a decade.

The pain reliever Aleve is a subtler sort of alteration.

Mitsubishi (whose Japanese name and symbol is three diamonds) knew that many travelers would recognize the Spanish word "Diamante" as the name of its luxury car.

These are all neologisms in English. And a far sight better than meaningless neologisms like "Amirage" or "Zixoryn."

See If the Name Is for Sale

Coors licensed the name of its upscale beer Irish Red from a long-defunct brewery.

Yves St. Laurent bought the name of its hot-selling fragrance Opium for only $200 from two elderly perfumers. But later they paid a million dollars for the right to the name Champagne. (It had already been cleared and registered in 70 countries.)

A bank paid $10,000 to acquire another bank's name for a cash management service no longer being marketed.

A *Fortune* 100 company acquired the rights to an automation software name from a Japanese competitor. One week of phone calls and faxes produced a letter of agreement.

So, if the name you covet is owned by someone else, go after it. It doesn't really matter whether the name is dormant or little used. Names are property, and they can be bought and sold just like real estate.

A few years back, for the first time, the House of Seagram sold the rights to a trademark, and for not much money. Why? According to the group's marketing director, Seagram had found it so hard to find a suitable name that it sought to buy a trademark and was treated in an accommodating way. So it returned the favor.

Here are some of the rules of the road for going after an existing name:

1. *You have nothing to lose by opening a channel of communication.* Remember that, when management says, "You want to do *what?*"

2. *Have an intermediary make the offer.* A good bet is a trademark attorney not already attached to your company. Pick one in a city near your target.

3. *Have a dollar sum in mind.* When these deals go, they often go quickly. What would that trademark be worth to you? Remember, its ownership has already been established and, probably, defended.

4. *Be certain the "assignment of rights" is perfectly clear.* Are you buying U.S. and Canadian rights only? Does the current owner retain any rights?

Watch for Changes in the Law

In 1989, the Federal trademark laws were liberalized so as to permit registrations for "intent to use." That opened the floodgates, and thousands of firms began to stockpile new names.

Treaty discussions are under way right now, around the globe, to change the rules governing trademark ownership. Part of the GATT treaty deals with names considered generic in the United States but hotly contested by Europeans.

Remember Ross Perot, squawking about "a giant sucking sound" as we supposedly lost jobs under NAFTA to cheaper Mexican labor? Well, nobody seemed to notice a *tiny* little sucking sound with a big impact on names.

Tucked into the NAFTA treaty is a clause that forbids the naming of a product with a "geographic brand name which is primarily misdescriptive" of the place from which it comes.

Meaning: You can no longer tap into that Idaho potato mystique by calling your spuds "Boise Brand Mashed Potatoes" unless they absolutely, positively come from Boise. No more "Santa Fe Salsa" if your picante actually comes from Paducah.

Says trademark attorney Michael Lasky: "I'll bet you two pesos that clients don't know these rules, and will insist on choosing such names because they did so in the past."

Think Multilingual

As the world goes global, the evidence continues to pile up that you'd better screen your name for multilingual suitability.

General Motors named a new Chevrolet "Beretta" without getting permission from the Italian arms manufacturer. It cost GM $500,000 to settle the lawsuit.

Estée Lauder was set to export its Country Mist makeup when German managers pointed out that in their language "mist" is slang for "manure." (The name became Country *Moist* in Germany.)

A food company advertised its giant burrito as a "Burrada." Big mistake. The colloquial meaning of that word *is* "big mistake"!

Now some of you are saying, "Not us. We'll never leave these shores." But what happens when the new boss decides to license your brand overseas? What happens when your division gets sold?

Imported names can be just as embarrassing. Do you think the Japanese coffee creamer "Creap" would make it here? Or the Scandinavian liquid "Super Piss" that unfreezes car locks? Or the Swiss/German chocolate candy bar named "Zit"?

To avoid sending your brand into an international nosedive, be sure you're acquainted with these four basic checkpoints.

1. *Acceptability.* Your name should be evaluated by a native-born person, fluent in the language of each foreign country

where you expect to do business. Does he or she regard the name as generally acceptable?

2. *Existing meaning.* Does your name have any similar or different meaning to the one you intend?

3. *Negative connotation.* What could your name be confused with?

4. *Pronounceability.* Is your name hard or easy to pronounce? (A genuine issue in Japan, for instance.)

A Universal Truth

Naming something may be the most universal aspect of being in business.

After all, you don't have to advertise, promote, package, do point-of-sale, or train for customer sensitivity. You don't even (perish the thought...) have to position yourself.

But whether it's your company, division, product, or service, you *do* have to call the baby something.

So why not choose a name that works overtime? A name that actually starts the positioning process.

In the Bible (Proverbs 22:1), it says, "A good name is rather to be chosen than great riches."

Who knows? Pick a good name, and you may be *doubly* blessed.

Getting Around
a Bad Name

There are times when, for a myriad of reasons, you're stuck with a bad name. (Maybe you received the U.S. distribution rights to a top foreign brand like Mukk Yogurt or Pocari Sweat soft drink.)

Or maybe you have a good corporate name that's bad for a new business. (Like "Xerox Computers.")

These are the most prevalent and difficult problems to resolve. Few companies ever see their name as being bad. And rarely do you find anyone with the courage to tell the chairman otherwise.

But if you can manage to defuse the internal problem, there are ways to get around a bad name.

Replacement

Option One is to summon some courage, march into the chairperson's office, and tell him or her that it's time to deep-six a name that's holding you back.

Your argument might go something like this: "Sure, our old name was a fine name. But it locks us into a past we've left behind. Sure, our old name has some equity. But not enough that it'll be missed. Sure, a few customers will be confused at first. But here's how we'll explain things to them."

The name "Harlem Savings Bank of New York" was holding the bank back from expanding, both outside of Harlem and outside of its existing customer base.

The cornerstone of the bank's strategy was a new name: Apple Bank. It severed old associations with Harlem. And it set up wholesome and friendly associations linked to the city's nickname, The Big Apple.

Resurrection

As we learned in Chapter 5, one can always bring back an old, well-known name.

House & Garden had been a leading decorating magazine for generations. Its name didn't make the earth move, but it was still a solid, understandable, meaningful name.

Then in 1987, in an attempt to draw a younger audience, the magazine was renamed *HG*. A trendy set of initials (a no-name name) suddenly replaced an 85-year-old name.

The results were disastrous. Cancellations poured in, and the magazine wobbled. *HG* was closed down in 1993.

Now comes word from Condé Nast Publications that it will resurrect the magazine and reintroduce it to a generation that is just discovering the pleasures of decorating and gardening. People in their thirties who just bought "the big house where they will be raising their children," according to Condé Nast's president.

The old/new magazine's name? *House & Garden*.

Moral: When you make a lousy call on a name, one option is to admit your blunder and turn back the clock.

Sub-branding

Another option is sub-branding.

Go down to your basement and take a look at the Dustbuster on the wall. What do you see? "Dustbuster" in big type. "Black & Decker" in small type.

The product's name is Dustbuster. Black & Decker is the maker, the brought-to-you-by name.

This is sub-branding, or sub-naming. The parent's name appears, but further down in the credits. The new offspring gets top billing.

With sub-branding, you're juggling two very different needs. You're keeping the corporate folks happy, because that proud old Black & Decker name is still right there. But you aren't turning off the consumer, because the potentially confusing name ("What's a power tool company doing with a mini-vacuum?") has been relegated to a lower billing.

V8 is brought to you by the Campbell Soup Company. But the bigger-than-life name on the bottle is, of course, V8. ("Campbell Vegetable Drink" wouldn't taste nearly as good.)

Courtyard and Residence Inns are both brought to you by Marriott. Same owner, very different levels of lodgings.

Two things happen with sub-branding.

First, the new name has a clearer path into the mind. Second, you avoid the messy confusion of locking an old name that already means something to a new product or service that stands for something else.

"Sneaky" Names

One group that appears to appreciate the importance of the name are those folks on the extreme right of the political spectrum.

Recognizing that a scary name like the Ku Klux Klan does not make for great public relations, today's rabble rousers go under some very tame and innocuous names.

Here's a sampling from a *Wall Street Journal* article on the subject:

The Historic Preservation Association (a fanatical foe of civil-rights groups), the Institute of Historical Review (publisher of articles denying the Holocaust) or the Council of Conservative Citizens (a publisher of many different government-aided conspiracy stories).

Moral: Be careful. You can't judge a group by its name.

The Isuzu Story

The most interesting and informative name story in recent years has been that of Isuzu Motors Ltd.

The saga of Isuzu started back in 1976, when Buick decided to replace its German Opels with Japanese ones.

The German mark was going through the roof at that time, and Buick thought they could get a better deal by doing business in Japanese yen.

To produce the new Japanese Opels, Buick turned to Isuzu, a company partially owned by Buick's parent. (In 1971, GM had bought 34 percent of Isuzu.)

How do you differentiate a Japanese Opel from a German one? That's a question that someone at Buick must have asked.

The decision was made to add the name of the manufacturer. The new Japanese cars would be called "Opel-Isuzu."

Bad name. Bad idea. In the ensuing years, millions of dollars were squandered trying to turn Isuzu into a big-selling import.

In Japanese, Isuzu means "fifty bells." The sound of 50 bells ringing is a pleasant one, conceptually. Unfortunately, in English, Isuzu doesn't sound like bells ringing. To Americans, Isuzu sounds more like a social disease than an automobile.

"How's Your Ol' Isuzu?"

"Name problems never die. They don't even fade away." The Isuzu story has once again proved this old adage.

The first sign of the name problem cropped up in the advertising prepared by Buick's ad agency. It made fun of the name. "What do Isuzus do?" asked one ad. "How's your ol' Isuzu?" inquired another.

Buick dealers were not amused. "The Isuzu name is disturbing and confusing," said a St. Louis dealer.

Was Buick management concerned about the name problem? Of course not. They were concerned about the supply problem. With first-year production of some 24,000 Isuzus planned for the U.S. market, they had hand-picked their dealer list to about 800 selected dealers.

"Alas, we have too few new Isuzus," ran the headline of one of the ads reporting on the thin supply situation.

Confidence ran high. "Dollar for dollar, the Opel Isuzu is more salable than the German Opel" said a Buick official.

Automotive News thought otherwise. Their May 31, 1976 issue reported that "Buick's Japanese import seems glued to the showroom floor."

Out of the planned production of 24,000 units, Buick dealers sold less than 8000 Opel Isuzus the first year.

By way of comparison, Buick dealers had sold 39,730 Opels the previous year.

It became painfully obvious to Buick management that their "ol' Isuzu" wasn't doing too well. So they did what they should have done in the first place: got rid of that ol' Isuzu name.

"Is it true what they say about Opel?" said the ads the following year. With that headline, you might think the copy would say, "We dropped the Isuzu name." But, no. The ads didn't mention that nasty word Isuzu.

Sales improved. 29,067 Japanese Opels were sold in 1977. But in 1978, sales dropped to 19,222. These were the years when the import market was booming. Toyota, Datsun, and Honda together sold well over a million cars in 1978.

Isuzu Goes Its Own Way

By the end of the decade, Isuzu had decided it could do better on its own. So the company set up American Isuzu Motors Inc., and hired a hot advertising agency headed by Jerry Della Femina, who was (ironically) the author of the book *From Those Wonderful Folks Who Gave You Pearl Harbor*.

The first year's advertising budget was $10 million, and the sales budget was for 35,000 vehicles. They easily made the ad budget, but missed the sales budget by a mile.

What was the theme of the advertising? The name problem, of course. "Isuzu. The advanced car with the backward name."

As you might have expected, the advanced car with the backward name failed to take off in the U.S. market. Instead of 35,000 vehicles, American Isuzu Motors managed to sell only 17,805 in 1981.

Sales dragged along until 1985, when the ad budget was upped to $22 million to counter the "disappointingly low" name awareness of Isuzu.

The ads keyed on the automaker's 69-year history, with the theme "The first car builders in Japan." One headline noted: "We're going to teach Nissan, Honda, and Toyota some respect for their elders."

That year Isuzu sold 26,953 cars. The "kids" sold 1,561,832, outselling their elders 58 to 1. Some respect.

Joe Isuzu Is Born

In the middle of 1986, Isuzu finally found what they thought had to be the answer to their "disappointingly low" name awareness. Actor David Leisure stood smiling in front of an Isuzu automobile and told TV viewers they could buy it for $9.

Liar Joe Isuzu was born.

The creative community went wild with joy, showering the

creators of Joe Isuzu with almost every industry award, including the 1987 Gold Lion at the International Advertising Film Festival at Cannes.

But all to no avail. Despite the creative acclaim, Isuzu car sales began to plummet. As the early nineties arrived, gigantic losses were registered.

The Sub-brand Solution

Isuzu has a name problem. Name problems never go away. The story is told about three guys chewing the fat. "I drive a Honda," says the first. "I drive a Toyota," says the second. "I drive a Japanese car" says the third, who, of course, is an Isuzu owner.

Who wants to admit they drive an Isuzu? It's a bad-sounding name. Remember the Edsel? It's a car that has something in common with the Isuzu.

Both have bad-sounding names, and bad-sounding names simply don't make it when it comes to personal products like automobiles.

But finally, Isuzu found a solution. Trucks and 4x4 vehicles are a different ball game. Logic suggests that a bad-sounding name won't hurt sales of these vehicles as much. Especially when you have another sub-brand to use, such as "Trooper." Recognizing this, Isuzu dropped their car line altogether and focused all their resources on Trooper and Rodeo.

Now, those are great names that an owner is proud to say. ("I own a Trooper," not "I own an Isuzu.")

The name problem has been solved, and business is a lot better. So much so that they can't make enough of those vehicles.

Never underestimate the value of having the right name. It can make you—and it sure can break you.

Naming a Category

This may surprise you, but a good bit of our time over the years has been spent figuring out exactly what it is that people are trying to sell. In other words, trying to name the the category.

Companies, large and small, have a very tough time describing their product, especially if it's a new category and a new technology.

Or else they describe it in terms that are very confusing, dooming the effort right out of the blocks.

The process of positioning a product in the mind must begin with what the product *is*. We sort and store information by category. That's why if you present a prospect with a confusing category, your chances of getting into his or her mind are slim to none.

What's a PDA?

Consider the problems that Apple encountered with the introduction of their Newton, a product they called a "PDA."

Right off the bat, their biggest positioning problem was: What are we selling?

The first print advertisements asked the question "What is a Newton?" The television commercials asked the questions "What is a Newton? Where is a Newton? Who is a Newton?"

Unfortunately, Apple failed to answer those questions in words that users felt comfortable in using.

PDA, or personal digital assistant, is not a category. Nor is there much hope in its *becoming* a category. (Pretty Damned Abstract is one tongue-in-cheek definition of PDA.)

Companies don't create categories. Users do. And so far, users haven't turned PDA into a category.

And you can't force the issue. Customers either are going to use your words, or they aren't. If they *don't*, you have to give up and look for a new category name.

Analyze What You've Got

Your first step, in deciding what you're selling, must be to articulate *what you've got* in terms so simple that a prospect or user can understand and repeat them.

For example, the Newton MessagePad is really three things: a computer, a communicator, and an electronic organizer.

While it does do all three things, it clearly will be difficult to build a position for a device that has so many functions.

This is often the problem that companies encounter, as they look for descriptions that will encompass all of the things a product does. This leads them down the path to complexity. And the more complex a description becomes, the tougher it gets for someone to figure out where to file this product in his or her mental file drawer.

Sacrifice Is Often Required

A better approach to the Newton positioning problem is *sacrifice*. (The essence of any effective strategy usually entails sacrifice.)

This doesn't mean Apple has to give up any of the Newton's functions. The product doesn't need to change, only the positioning. But which function should the positioning focus on?

Not the computer function. If the Newton were positioned as a pen computer, you'd be taking a step backwards. While the older generation might see the advantages of a pen computer, the younger generation would not. Most younger people would rather use a keyboard than a pen.

Not the communications function. (Where's the phone?) Furthermore, the fax function has limitations until the infrastructure is in place.

This leaves the organizer function as the only viable Newton function to build a position around. Interestingly, if you ask current users of Newton why they use the device, they'll say, "for the organizer function."

And there seems to be a relatively high level of satisfaction, among Newton users, for the product as an organizing tool.

Make an Enemy

Every marketing program has to have a marketing enemy. As a "PDA," the Newton had no enemies. It also had no category, and no business.

But as an "organizer" it had a great deal of competition, especially from the Sharp Wizard.

The market for electronic organizers is enormous. In 1994 more than 10 million electronic organizers were sold, as compared to 120,000 personal digital assistants. And Sharp sold about 60 percent of the organizers.

Segment the Category

Often, the best move is not to try to coin a new category name but to segment an existing category. That's a quick and easy way to gain entry into the mind. (Tandem did this with "fault-tolerant computers," as did Orville Redenbacher with "gourmet popping corn.")

The obvious way for Apple to do this would be to reposition the Newton as "the ultimate organizer."

In *Marketing Warfare,* we call such a position "a high-end flanking strategy."

Actually, the high price of the Newton is helpful in establishing this position. In essence, you are creating a new high-price segment of an existing category. Much as Montblanc did in pens, Rolex in watches, and Mercedes-Benz in automobiles.

Also, being able to write your notes, rather than having to use one of those pygmy keyboards, certainly says that the Newton is a big improvement over the traditional organizer.

Confess Your Sins

If by chance you have to undo a bad category decision in a new-product launch, the best way to do it is to be as candid and honest as you can.

Admit that your product turned out to be something other than what you planned. If you do this, your prospect will be much more willing to accept your repositioning strategy.

Apple could generate a lot of interest by running an ad that says something like: "Inadvertently, we made the Wizard obsolete."

That would sell a lot more Newtons than their "What's a Newton?"

Negative Generic Names

You have to be careful not to get saddled with a negative generic name.

In the ever-changing world of television services, there is now a form of service called a "Multipoint Microwave Distribution System," or MMDS for short. I won't go into the technology, other than to say it's a tower that beams a signal to a small antenna mounted on your house. The signal can carry the major cable television channels. It delivers an excellent picture, with no cable strung from house to house.

But because of the long name, the unofficial generic name became "wireless cable." To many, the word *wireless* says "convenient," not "better." (Wired phones work better than wireless phones.)

So suddenly you have a problem of being perceived as 'the poor man's cable." That is, cable that isn't quite as good as the real thing.

Negative names can stick, so unless this name is replaced with a new generic, long-term success is a long shot.

Figuring Out a New Generic

When faced with the tough task of coming up with a new generic, you should start with a simple analysis of how a new product works, then try to use those words. When the automobile was born, it was christened a "horseless carriage." (A simple description of how it works.) "Cable television" accurately describes how that system works.

The product we're now discussing beams waves of video signals to a small antenna. So the obvious new generic that emerges is that of "videowave television," or VTV for short.

That's a lot better than "MMDS," or "wireless cable," especially when you consider the fact that the company's name is Videotron. Get it? Videotron Videowave Television is a neat memory device. (See Chapter 15 on names.)

(P.S.: If it ever comes to your neighborhood, get it. It's got some neat features.)

The Bigger the Business, the Better

When you're defining your business, try to present it in its broadest terms. This will tend to make it more impressive. If you're going to own an idea, you may as well own as *big* an idea as possible.

This was the case at a Silicon Valley company I visited some years back, called Silicon Graphics.

As is so often the case, their problem was that of defining their business. They had invented what they called "3-D Computing." This was no easy task, as it called for advanced computer chips to deal with images rather than numbers or words. Also, they had to find a way to *move* those images, so as to create a sense of reality on the computer screen. The answer lay in a unique "Geometry Engine" technology, which does the intricate mathematics required.

But on top of all that, they had to develop the complex software tools that would enable 3-D applications to be developed. The early heavy users were in Hollywood. They used Silicon Graphics equipment to generate many of their dramatic visual effects. Also, laboratories were simulating and evaluating accidents. Pilots were learning to fly on the ground. Engineers were simulating products.

They had a big business idea, but could it be bigger?

The "Visual Computing" Company

Interestingly, when we analyzed their business we found that their unique technology allowed computers to work in color, motion, and three dimensions in real time.

What their business was, in the broadest terms, was "visual computing." They were the pioneers in a field that would do for images what word processing has done for the typed word.

And as prices came down, we could foresee an enormous future in a number of larger applications such as desktop publishing, package design, manufacturing, and even multimedia. (At the moment they're working on "video on demand," which could be the ultimate visual-computing problem.)

This redefinition makes "3-D computing" their credentials, and "visual computing" their wider business. And today, Silicon Graphics is certainly a far bigger company than it was in the old "3-D" days.

The "Contact Software" Company

Probably the most interesting "naming the category" story we have come across is that of a company once called Conductor Software.

Pat Sullivan, the CEO, and his associates came to us one day in 1988, and we discovered that we weren't talking software for musicians, but software for salespeople.

The product was called ACT, because they figured they were selling a "Business Activity Manager" product. But then, Lotus was pushing PIM, which was a "Personal Information Manager."

They just weren't sure what kind of information they were selling. And with sales of less than a million dollars a year, they weren't selling a lot.

What it turned out they *were* selling was software that enabled salespeople to manage their many contacts. They were "the leading contact-manager software company."

They Changed Their Name

Now that they had a better handle on what they were selling, they gave themselves a better handle. Conductor Software became Contact Software International, and they were off to the races.

They tied in with the big laptop manufacturers and

became the hot laptop software. (Laptops, after all, are the salesperson's computer of choice.)

By 1993, sales had risen to $20 million. In fact, things were going so nicely that Pat Sullivan and company sold out, to the tune of $47 million.

That's not bad for a company that, five years earlier, wasn't even sure what they were selling.

Research Can Confuse You

The question you're asking yourself is, "Don't you believe in research?"

The answer is yes and no.

We believe in certain *kinds* of research. We also believe in not getting mesmerized by data, in not trusting your customers to give you all the answers, and in trusting your own instincts. To help us with these likes and dislikes, we return to the military analogy we employed in our second book, *Marketing Warfare.*

The parallels between war and marketing are numerous.

In business, the terrain is the marketplace. The enemy is the competition. The objective is the consumer's mind. The weapons are the media.

Research Is "Intelligence"

And the gathering of intelligence is known as "research."

Good military brains are often suspicious of the intelligence reports they receive. (And rightly so.) So are many marketers.

Our hero, the famous military historian Karl von Clausewitz, put it this way: "A great part of the information obtained in war is contradictory, a still greater part is false, and by far the greatest part is of a doubtful character."

Can't live with it, can't live without it, you might say.

But whatever its intrinsic frustrations, intelligence gathering is continually broadening in scope. Companies such as GM, Kodak, and Motorola have established formal intelligence units, to oversee their intelligence work. Other companies have made "business intelligence" and "competitor analysis" a key part of their strategic planning process.

America's 50 leading research organizations spent $4.1 billion. Thirty-eight percent came from outside the United States.

These intelligence efforts are growing in direct proportion to competitive pressures.

A Fundamental Paradox

That's probably because of a fundamental paradox in human behavior. The more unpredictable the world becomes, the more we seek out and rely upon forecasts to determine what we should do. (The *California Management Review* made this point in a landmark article entitled "Management & Magic.")

Gone are the days when companies designed their strategies as if they had no competition. Gone are the strategic planners who crunched numbers, preached quantitative models, but ignored the guys who were prepared to eat their lunch. (When growth in many markets stalled in the early 1990s, and competition escalated, the grandiose strategies of the day suddenly weren't worth the paper they were printed on.)

So what's a marketer to do? How can you best use intelligence to make sound strategic decisions?

Here are some suggestions.

Study Thy Competitor

Who do you suppose were the first folks to pay $1950 for a 200-page study of Sears' financial services operations?

Citicorp, Bank of America, Prudential, and G.E. Credit, that's who.

They were simply heeding the single most important dictum of marketing intelligence: Study thy competitor.

Today, a strategy plan looks more like a battle plan for dealing with the enemy. It dissects each participant's current and future stance, on everything from manufacturing costs and technology to plant capacity and distribution channels.

And today's battle plan includes a list of strengths and weaknesses, as well as courses of action to either exploit them or defend against them.

You can always get a handle on what your business rivals are planning. The cardinal rule of intelligence is "Wherever money is being exchanged, so is information," according to Leonard Fuld, a specialist in business research and author of *The New Competitor Intelligence.*

Study Thy Competitor *Some More*

The ultimate plan even contains a dossier on each of the competitors' key marketing people. It reveals their favorite tactics and styles of operation. (Not unlike the profiles the Germans kept on Allied commanders during World War II.)

Hollywood loves a good script, too. So, in the movie version of his life, Patton says of Rommel (in the heat of battle), "I *read your book,* you son of a bitch!"

Like nations at war, corporations have cultures too. Their leaders have individual styles. Is she bold? Is he conservative? How will each react to a potential move?

Says Clausewitz: "It is from the character of our adversary's position that we can draw conclusions as to his designs."

Don't Get Mesmerized by the Data

In our over-communicated society, the problem is too much raw data, rather than not enough.

One of the pitfalls of the multibillion dollar marketing research industry is that researchers don't get paid for simplicity. Instead, they seem to get paid by the pound.

The need is to filter out the overabundance of data and focus on the significant pieces. Usually, those represent less than 5 percent of your entire information inventory. Two true stories may be in order.

The scene: The office of a brand manager at Procter & Gamble. Our problem was, what to do with one of their largest brands. We asked a simple question as to the availability of their research. Once again we were surprised by the answer: "Research? We've got a computer full of it. How do you want it? In fact, we've got so much of it that we don't know what to do with it."

The scene: The research cubicle of a 300-bed hospital in a Midwestern city. The cup ranneth over. There were awareness surveys, employee surveys, employer surveys, staff physician surveys, nonaligned physician surveys, new-patient surveys, old-patient surveys, new-service surveys, and expansion studies. (Do you wonder if there was any marketing money left over to actually *do* something?)

A flood of data should never be allowed to wash away your common sense, and your own feeling for the market.

And remember that fads can masquerade as data. According to one market estimate in 1980, 5 percent of all U.S. households would be hooked into Videotext by 1985. But Videotext was the fad that never was. Knight-Ridder spent $60 million setting up a Videotext service that never made money and was ultimately abandoned.

Don't Get Mesmerized by Focus Groups

Focus groups are one of the most popular and misused research tools in the business. Allowing rooms full of total strangers with big mouths to influence your marketing strategy can be disastrous.

First of all, the process has been distorted. Have you ever wondered where the word *focus* came from? It was first used in the '60s as a way to better focus the ensuing research on a subject. That's right, it was just the first step.

Yet today, many companies never get around to the quantitative research, based on a true sample of the target audience. They act on the opinions blurted out by those small groups of people.

Secondly, the process turns casual bystanders (or "bysitters") into marketing experts.

The average person doesn't think too deeply about anything much beyond money, sex, gossip, and their weight. The average person hasn't really *thought* about toothpaste for a total of 10 minutes in his or her lifetime. Much less for the two hours of a toothpaste focus group. And yet in a focus group, you're asking people to form opinions in a manner that goes way beyond that of their normal mental processing.

You're turning them into marketing managers for a day. They'll be only too happy to tell you how to run your business. The question is, should you *let* them?

Focus Groups Are a Powderkeg

They can blow up, and blow you off in the wrong direction.

Ask women about beauty products in a group setting, and typically they will deny any emotional involvement. Instead, they'll tell you what they think you want to hear. The same with men and automobiles.

Ask people to critique your strategies or your advertising, and they'll overstate their motivations and needs and understanding.

Focus groups are balky barometers of behavior. When a big

packaged-goods company planned to introduce a squirtable soft-drink concentrate for kids, it held focus groups to watch the reaction. In the sessions, children squirted the product neatly into cups. But back home, few of the little rascals could resist the temptation to decorate the floors and walls with the colorful liquid. After a flood of complaints from parents, the product was withdrawn.

Don't Get Mesmerized by Test Markets

There's a Catch-22 factor at work in test markets. They are meant to forecast product performance, but results can be skewed by unforeseen events in the marketplace. Campbell Soup Company spent 18 months developing a blended fruit juice called Juiceworks. By the time it reached the market, three competing brands were already on store shelves. Campbell dropped the product. (Did they remember to "study thy competitors"?)

When Crystal Pepsi was test-marketed, it quickly moved to over a four share, and was just as quickly christened by the trade press as a success. Wrong. Several months later it plunged to a one share. What the marketing people forgot to factor in was the curiosity factor. People were curious about a clear cola, but then decided brown colas taste better. (No surprise.)

Don't Believe Everything They Say

Researchers may promise to reveal attitudes, but attitudes aren't a reliable predictor of behavior. People often talk one way, but act another.

Forty years ago, DuPont commissioned a study in which interviewers stopped 5000 women on their way into supermarkets and asked them what they expected to buy.

If you had gone to the bank on those findings alone, you would have been deeply in hock.

How come? Because interviewers then checked the same women's purchases on their way *out* of the store. In terms of the product categories they had expected to purchase, only 3 of 10 bought the specific brand they had said they would. Seven out of 10 had bought other brands.

Another classic example is the research conducted before Xerox introduced the plain-paper copier. What came back was the conclusion that no one would pay 5¢ for a plain-paper copy when they could get a Thermofax copy for a cent and a half.

Xerox ignored the research, and the rest is history.

Get Some Snapshots of the Mind

What you really want to get is a quick snapshot of the *perceptions* that exist in the mind. Not deep thoughts, not suggestions.

What you're after are the perceptual strengths and weaknesses of you and your competitors, as they exist in the minds of the target group of consumers.

Our favorite mode of research is to line up the basic attributes that surround a category and then ask people to score them on a rating scale of 1 to 10. This is done on a competitor-by-competitor basis. The objective is to see who owns what idea or concept in a category.

Take toothpaste as an example. There are perhaps six attributes that surround this product: cavity prevention, taste, whitening, breath protection, natural ingredients, and advanced technology. Crest built their brand on cavity protection, Aim on taste, UltraBrite on whitening, and Close-Up on breath protection. More recently, Tom's of Maine has pre-empted natural ingredients, and Mentadent has become a major player with its baking soda and peroxide technology.

Everyone owns an attribute.

The trick is to figure out in advance which attribute you would like to preempt in the mind. The research should serve as your road map into that mind, and around your competitors' perceptions.

See Which Way the Battle Is Going

There's a story told about the drunk and the lamppost and the marketer.

The drunk, you see, was using the lamppost for support, rather than for illumination. How was the marketer using the research?

Research is intended to illuminate the scene. Not to support the idea of the moment. And certainly not to neatly solve your problem.

Acclaimed historian Barbara Tuchman said:

> Most men will not believe what does not fit in with their plans or suit their prearrangements. The flaw in all intelligence is that it is no better than the judgment of its interpreter, and this judgment is the product of a mass of individual, social, financial, and political bias, prejudgment, and wishful thinking.

One of the toughest assignments for a marketer today is to see where the war is going, not just where it has been.

"Boldness becomes rarer, the higher the rank," says Clausewitz.

It takes a bold marketer to rise above the built-in prejudices of the way we all look at research and intelligence.

The Positioning Power of PR

Companies in America presently drop more than a billion dollars on their public relations efforts.

That's not chopped liver. But most of these programs aren't positioning programs. They're "name in the press" programs that are measured in about the same way as you would chopped liver: by the pound.

The Column-Inch Trap

Public relations is hard to measure. The most widely accepted method is the avoirdupois (literally, "goods by weight") approach. Clippings are collected and submitted to managements. Audiotapes and videotapes are edited together into long reels. Content is largely irrelevant. *Weight* is all that counts.

Fortunately, management doesn't pay close enough attention. If a report seems to weigh in at the acceptable number of troy ounces, the job is officially pronounced "well done."

But a public relations report can be light in weight and heavy in effectiveness, if each press penetration supports and reinforces the position.

Positioning in PR

In spite of its overwhelming acceptance by the advertising community, it's possible that positioning will come to play an even greater role in public relations.

The reason is obvious. Positioning is essentially an "against" strategy. That is, you normally position your company or brand *against* another.

And as every editor knows, what you stand *for* is not news. What you're *against* is the thing that makes news. Ralph Nader became famous not by advocating safer cars but by singlehandedly attacking the world's largest corporation. Unfortunately for Ralph, he's "against" virtually everything. He has become predictable, lost all his news value, and become invisible.

Bad news for Mr. Nader, because as veteran newsman Daniel Schorr says: "In this mass communications society, if you don't exist in the media, for all practical purposes you don't exist."

Being against an idea or concept (not necessarily another company) is an equity that can be translated into publicity coverage. Editors encourage controversy. Readers and viewers soak it up. Controversy is a tool that can drive your message into the mind. Never be afraid to exploit it. As advertising guru David Ogilvy once acknowledged, "Roughly six times as many people read the average article as the average advertisement. Editors communicate better than ad men."

Needed: Marketing Objectives

In the past, however, many PR programs haven't been effective from a marketing point of view. And it's easy to see why. In PR, your inherent lack of control over what is being printed or said about you often leads to a lack of direction. As one grizzled PR veteran defines things: "Advertising is what you pay for. PR is what you *pray* for."

The discipline that positioning can bring to a publicity program can make an enormous difference in terms of results.

To make positioning work in PR, however, the emphasis has to shift from "getting your name in the paper" to achieving marketing objectives.

(Many prominent companies don't need more exposure. They need less but better-directed exposure in the media.)

In the PR business, anonymity is a resource. It can easily be squandered by too much publicity. An unknown company with an unknown product has much more to gain from PR than an old company with an established product.

"You never get a second chance," someone once said, "to make a good first impression."

Publicity is like eating. Nothing kills the appetite quite as much as a hearty meal. And nothing kills the PR potential of a product quite as much as a premature feature story. Or a misdirected television placement.

Publicity First; Advertising Second

Unplanned, untimely exposure dulls the publicity potential of a new product or concept.

The general rule is: PR first, advertising second. (PR plants the seed. Advertising harvests the crop.)

The truth is, advertising can't start a fire. It can only fan a fire after its been started. To get something out of nothing, you need the validity that third-party endorsements bring.

It's like going to your neighborhood nerd and asking him what computer you should buy. His advice will be worth a lot more than all the ads you've seen, because he's "objective." (No axes to grind.)

When a company is using positioning as its basic advertising strategy, then it simply makes sense to use positioning strategy in its PR. Especially since the PR ought to precede the advertising.

Samuel Adams beer was a small business that couldn't afford advertising but could position itself as a high-quality local brew. It won taste tests in Boston, then graduated to win the National Beer Tasteoff in Denver, getting major publicity all the way.

Those credentials, and the third-party endorsements, have paid off. Today Sam Adams has a multimillion-dollar advertising budget. And it all started with PR.

Too often, this never happens. Advertising agencies and public relations agencies see themselves as competitors. For the client's ear, and his or her dollar. Internal departments compete in the same way.

This intramural rivalry saps the strength of many product and corporate programs. The advertising runs too soon, and kills much of the PR potential. And the PR lacks a positioning concept, so it doesn't set up anything that the advertising can exploit.

What's needed is a basic change in the way advertising and public relations programs are planned. Programs should be *linear* rather than *spatial*.

Quick Bang versus Slow Buildup

In a special program, the elements start together, but in different space. (Public relations, advertising, sales promotion, etc.) This is the typical way most programs are conceived. The quick bang, if you will.

But when the smoke clears away, when the excitement of the initial launch is over, usually nothing has changed. The prospect's attitude is the same as it was before.

In a linear program, the elements unfold over a period of time. The advantage, of course, is that they can work together to reinforce each other. The slow buildup that leads to a big change in the prospect's mind.

The trouble with most spatial programs is that they don't *go* anywhere. There's no unfolding of elements, no drama, no "What's going to happen next?" excitement. No climax.

Which is why the beginning of a new year usually marks the start of a new spatial program. With new objectives, new strategy, new advertising theme.

This annual changeover is the very reverse of good positioning strategy. More than anything else, successful positioning requires "consistency." You must keep at it, year after year after year.

A linear program helps you to achieve this consistency. The gradual buildup of an idea or concept provides plenty of time for the public relations portion of the program to be fully developed.

The Lotus Linear Program

The Lotus repositioning program that was described in Chapter 8 is a classic example of putting PR first, advertising second.

Over a number of months, the press established "groupware" as an important development, with the success of Notes as the proof of its growing importance. A review of some of the business press headlines dramatically makes the point:

The Wall Street Journal: "Lotus Development Relies on Notes to Write Success. Firm Stresses Not-So-New **Groupware** Product That Is Finally Catching On."

Fortune: "**Groupware** Can Get Everyone in a Company into the Act."

Business Week: "Lotus Notes Gets a Lot of Notice. Users Praise '**Groupware**' and Rivals Scramble to Catch Up."

Information Week: "**Groupthink** Takes Hold. Lotus Crows as Microsoft and WordPerfect Bow to Notes."

Fortune: "Why Microsoft Can't Stop Lotus Notes."

The advertising for Notes didn't really start until 1994, two years after the start of the PR.

The PR lit the fire and started the repositioning process.

No-Load versus Load Mutual Funds

One of the lesser-known marketing battles in America might be dubbed The Mutual Fund Wars. It is being waged between the funds sold by brokers (load funds) and those sold direct via advertising (no-load funds).

We were asked in on behalf of the brokers. Even before we got to the first meeting, we knew the essence of the brokers' problem. Simply, they had allowed the terminology of load versus no-load to be established.

This immediately ceded the moral high ground to the no-loads.

Defending broker commissions could be interpreted as trying to justify unnecessary or exorbitant fees. That's not a comfortable spot to be in.

Prospects want to believe they can buy a mutual fund for nothing.

Change the Question

The only real strategy open to the broker-sold load funds was to segment the market and change the question. We call this a "narrow the focus" strategy.

The trick was to exploit the difference between the active, do-it-yourself investors and the more passive, I'm-not-so-sure investors.

Give up the active investors to the no-loads. Aggressively pursue the passive investors as the best prospects.

So the strategy became:

In mutual funds, the question isn't load or no-load.

In mutual funds, the question is help versus no help.

The key was to admit that some people don't need much help. They have the time, knowledge, and interest to work their way through the 4000 funds.

But others do need help analyzing performance numbers, help keeping track of trends, and help with their personal investment needs.

The sum-up thought: Broker-sold mutual funds are loaded with *help*.

Needed: Third-Party Credentials

This was a positioning program that needed an aggressive PR program to establish the "help" strategy. That's why the first thing the group did was to establish a "Mutual Fund Forum" whose objective was to use public relations to better inform the investing public about the help versus no-help issue.

The early results show the power of a positioning-directed PR program:

Financial Planning: "Mutual fund investing is simple, but it's also very sophisticated. Now is the time to give investors some **help**."

National Underwriter: "The aim of the program of the new organization is to **clarify** an increasingly **complex** mutual fund market."

New York Newsday: "Financial advisors and planners can **help** those without the time or knowledge to pick through the 5000 funds on the market."

The Detroit News: "Qualified financial advisors make it their **full-time job to stay on top** of market shifts, portfolios, and changing client needs."

Boston Herald: "We agree there isn't a lot of difference per se in load vs. no-load funds. What we really think the issue should be is whether the investor needs **help or no help**."

As you can see, the brokers are beginning to get some "help" from the press.

The Media Taketh Away

Third-party endorsements don't come with lifetime guarantees. What the media giveth, the media can taketh away.

Consider high and mighty Intel Corp., the darling of the press, the business schools, the financial community, and the computer crowd. And a mega-advertiser to boot.

Intel's astounding—and arrogant—response to the flawed Pentium chip turned a technical problem into a PR nightmare.

How did they blunder? Initially, Intel denied that the problem existed. When irrefutable evidence was presented that the problem did exist, they downplayed its significance. Then their acclaimed CEO claimed that no one had told him how bad things were.

At last, they reluctantly agreed to replace the flawed chips. But it was a little late.

The press had a field day ripping into the once-sacred Intel. First the trade press, then the scientific press, then the business and financial press, then the mainstream national consumer media. (Usually, just the kind of media buildup one wants!)

Quietly, later, Intel lowered prices on the Pentium chip.

The lessons? 1) Your position is never sacrosanct with the media. 2) Everybody loves to see the big guy take a fall.

Don't ignore your reputation, responsibility, or credibility. If you abuse it, you lose it.

On the Other Hand . . .

If you grasp the reality and severity of a crisis, take charge quickly, and move decisively, you can mobilize the media (and more) to take your side.

Consider the potential damage of a sweeping product recall. In the summer of 1993, all 400,000 owners of Saturn automobiles faced a recall of nearly everything Saturn had produced. Repair was needed on a faulty wire that could short out and start an engine fire. The cost to the company was more than $11 million, but the repair was free to owners. And the voluntary recall was handled with precision and intelligence.

Company executives raced to control the damage to Saturn's fledgling image by appearing on television to explain the problem. The company authorized dealers to spend money on food, refreshments, loaner cars, courtesy transportation, and even repairs at the homes of owners who couldn't get to dealerships.

The recall, in fact, was turned into a customer-satisfaction blitz that became a perfect example of Saturn's reason for being.

So if you abuse it, you lose it.

But if you coddle it, you can keep it.

Six
Positioning Pitfalls

In the 15 or so years since I cowrote *Positioning: The Battle for Your Mind*, I've seen a *lot* go wrong with even the best-laid plans. So this time around, it will be worth spending some time on just what *can* go wrong in developing and maintaining a positioning strategy.

Here are the six positioning pitfalls that are at the heart of many failed programs.

1. The Obvious Factor

Most positioning concepts are painfully obvious. In fact, we often say that the process is a search for the obvious. What is obvious inside the company will also be obvious in the minds of the customers and prospects.

Coca-Cola's obvious position is that of "the Real Thing." They invented the category to make every other cola seem like a copy. That's the obvious idea they should use forever. "Always Coca-Cola" is nothing but wishful thinking. In fact, in terms of supermarket sales, half the time it's always *Pepsi*-Cola.

So why does Coca-Cola keep drifting away from its obvious strategy? Because unfortunately, the marketing mind tends to think that the obvious is too simple. Not clever enough. Also, because obvious ideas tend to hang around a company for a long while, they don't seem exciting. They're old hat.

KPMG Peat Marwick was well aware of the fact of their

global leadership. They just never saw it as a positioning strategy. Too obvious.

Likewise, Lotus was well aware of the groupware idea. There it was, in *Business Week* magazine. All we did was point it out and show them how to use it.

Carvel had the "Ice Cream Bakery" strategy in hand. They just weren't sure that was really it. Too simple.

Much of positioning is basic common sense. The problem is that marketers don't trust common sense as much as they trust some complex piece of research.

Don't be afraid to embrace the obvious.

2. The Future Factor

Many powerful positioning ideas founder on the future.

In other words, while a company sees the value of a strategy for today's and tomorrow's business, they aren't so sure it will hold up all the way into the future. They want an idea that will be able to accommodate some future yet still unformulated plan.

Once, in a roomful of Xerox technical management people, I was pushing the future of laser printing as a big business. "Lasography" as a follow-on to "Xerography."

After the presentation, some senior engineer stood up and declared that laser printing was old hat. They had been working on it for a number of years. What they needed was an idea that encompassed the present as well as the future. When I politely asked what the future held, he proudly announced "Ion deposition."

All I could say was, "Let's do 'Lasography' today, and when you're ready you can do 'Ionography.'" (All that remark did was to make me out to be a wise-ass. End of sale.)

Finding success today is what you must first worry about. If you do that, your chances will be greatly enhanced that you'll have some money to spend on tomorrow.

One observation I've heard a lot is, "I don't want to be niched. I want to keep my future options open."

Believe me, if you *don't* get niched in the customer's mind, your future options will be quite limited.

3. The Cutesy Factor

Don't be cute. Tell it like it is. What's most painful is to see a company go through the strategic process and come up with a simple positioning statement, then turn it over to the creative folks and watch them get cute with it.

Powerful ideas tend to tell it like it is. They're straight, not cute.

Volkswagen's "Think small" was as straight as an arrow.

Volvo's "Drive safely" is simple and direct.

Today, the famous No. 2 Avis campaign that was once called a "creative breakthrough" looks like it was taken right out of a business plan: "Avis is No. 2 in rent-a-cars. So why go with us? We try harder."

The current Hertz program is just as brilliant in its directness: "In rent-a-cars, there's Hertz and not exactly."

That's telling it like it is.

Once, while working with a bank on their strategy, I discovered that they were the leader in Small Business Administration loans in their trading area. Most of those loans, it turned out, were going to recent immigrants starting businesses in America. People pursuing the American dream of success.

The recommended positioning strategy was simple and direct. This bank was "the home of the American dream."

Everyone liked the idea, and it was handed over to an agency for implementation. When I saw it again it had become: "We bank on your dreams."

Cute . . . *but not exactly.*

4. The Would-Be Hero Factor

Would-be heroes can be an enormous problem for a positioning strategy. This is especially true in large organizations where you have a number of people vying for the CEO's attention.

These are the people who measure every decision against their own personal agendas before they view it against the company agenda. The questions they ask themselves are things like: Will it make me look good? Will I get the credit? If it fails, will I look bad?

This type of attitude produces what I call "inside-out thinking." Decisions are made on the basis of what's going on inside the organization. For positioning thinking to succeed, it really has to be "outside in." In other words, you're making your decisions based on what's going on outside, in the marketplace.

As management maven Peter Drucker once wrote: "What business am I in? The question can be answered only by looking at the business from the outside, from the point of view of the customer and the market."

Would-be heroes are subjective. Good marketing people are objective.

Subjective decisions tend to be lousy decisions, since they're often long on wishful thinking and short on reality. Here's how to spot would-be heroes, as well as some tips on getting around them before they have a chance to do in your program.

They generally come in two species.

The New Shooter

Chances are that when a new CEO or department head arrives, you're looking at a would-be hero. Obviously, any piece of thinking that was around before he or she arrived is suspect. I can't tell you how many positioning programs have been wiped out because the new shooter wanted his/her own solution to the problem, in order to "look good."

The questions that you're asked after you've shown your program are generally the best tipoff that you're dealing with this type of person. If you hear, "Have you researched that?" or "Have you looked at other ideas?" your program may well be in trouble.

Your only chance to avoid this kind of pitfall is to try *not* to sell your ideas. In fact, I advise that you deliberately undersell them by indicating that this strategy wasn't well received by the executive who was replaced. That way, you give the new shooter a chance to be a hero by honoring a piece of thinking that others had ignored.

The Ladder Climber

If you're working away on your brand and, suddenly, some executive from on high lobs a strategic idea into your office, you may have a "ladder climber" on your hands.

Most likely this is a would-be hero who senses that he or she needs a high-visibility move to get the top job, and therefore contributes a "big idea" to your efforts. Since it's inside-out thinking, it's probably a lousy idea. So be careful of these "contributions." They can be live grenades. They can go off in your face.

The trick is to find a way to disarm them before they can do any damage. One way to do this is to bring in outsiders to evaluate the higher-up's strategy, thus keeping yourself out of harm's way. (Ladder climbers get very upset with junior executives who say no to their ideas.)

This was precisely the scenario when we were asked to review a strategic problem at one of America's largest packaged-goods companies. We went through the exercise and presented our advice. En route, we discredited a high-level executive's idea. It was never heard of again.

Unfortunately, this story doesn't have a happy ending. The brand manager had our presentation videotaped, and distributed the tape around the organization. This probably embarrassed the ladder climber, having his idea dismissed in such a very public way.

Our guy's phone went dead, and he was never heard from again. That videotape went off in his face.

5. The Numbers Factor

If you live by the numbers, you die by the numbers.

These days, Wall Street often is the enemy of effective marketing. With their short-term-earnings focus, companies get bullied into doing enormous damage to themselves in their efforts to show ever-increasing percentage gains in sales and profits.

Positioning is a long-term, not a short-term process. It takes time and money to do the job. If you don't build these elements into the program, you simply won't succeed.

Nothing illustrated this problem better for me than a session I had with a division of one of America's preeminent drug companies.

My assignment was to spend several days in a group meeting of their marketing folks, kibitzing the following year's marketing plans. Asking stupid but obvious questions.

One bright young person stood up and started in with his 15 percent sales-increase objective. Then, in almost the same breath, he talked about the arrival of some new, very difficult competition.

I stopped him right there, and quizzed him on exactly how sales were going to increase in that kind of competitive environment. His answer was some line extension, new flavors, and a little tinkering.

When pressed about these efforts, he admitted that his sales-increase figure wasn't realistic, but said that his boss's boss had made him put that number into his plan. (I began to smell Wall Street.)

Because of the stir I caused, three weeks later I received a call from the boss's boss. He wanted to sit in on a similar session. The same stuff happened, only this time the big boss took me aside and quietly explained that all this was being caused by *his* boss, the CEO. (Now I *knew* it was Wall Street!)

Marketing is an exercise in *reality*. You can't let what the numbers people *want* you to earn affect your decisions. Going up every year isn't realistic. Sometimes, given the stiff competition out there, just staying even is a major accomplishment.

Implementing endless product variations, just to pump sales, only clutters the shelves and shifts the balance of power to the retailer who owns the shelf space. (Consider the cough/cold aisle in your average supermarket. There are so many variations you can't even find what you're looking for.)

Running out endless line extensions just to get bigger numbers only mucks up brand perceptions and opens the door for specialized competition. The beer business has regular, light, draft, dry, and now ice beers. It's no wonder the only growth is in the microbrewery segment.

Get your positioning and your programs implemented properly, and the numbers will come. But you've got to have some patience.

6. The Tinkering Factor

The road to chaos is paved with improvements.

In all my years in the business, I've never seen a marketing person come into a new assignment, look around, and say, "Things look pretty good. Let's not touch a thing."

To the contrary. All red-blooded marketing people want to get in there and start improving things. They want to make their mark. Just *sitting there* wouldn't feel right.

When a company has offices full of marketing people, you've got to expect endless tinkering with a brand. It's how they keep from getting bored.

Someone on the Prell Shampoo brand says, "Hey, why don't we add a blue Prell to our line of green Prell?" Of course this ignores the consumer perception that if it isn't green, it can't be Prell.

Bad idea.

Someone on the Pepsi brand says, "Hey, why don't we take advantage of the new-age purity fad, and introduce a clear Pepsi? We'll call it Crystal Pepsi." Of course this ignores the consumer perception that if it isn't brown, it's not going to taste like a cola.

Bad idea.

At McDonald's someone says, "Hey, let's take advantage of the pizza trend and add McPizza to the menu!" Of course this ignores the consumer perception that hamburger joints can't know much about making pizza.

Bad idea.

Someone at Anheuser-Busch says, "Hey, why don't we add dry and ice beers to our lineup?" Of course this ignores the consumer perception that beer is usually wet and not served over ice.

Bad ideas.

Positioning has to line up with the perceptions in the mind, not go against them. What people inside the company perceive as "improvements" only cause confusion inside the mind of the prospect.

In positioning, once you've gotten a brand up to altitude, your watchword should be "steady as she goes."

The Right People
in the Room

In one of my many strategic meetings at one of America's largest companies, a young lady presented what I consider one of the most important pieces of advice I have ever received about positioning.

At the end of a presentation, she came over and offered congratulations on what she thought was an excellent piece of thinking.

But then she startled me by saying that I would never sell any of my positioning ideas. When I asked why, she replied with a simple but brilliant observation: "You'll never have the right people in the room."

She went on to explain that the top people don't go to meetings like this. And powerful ideas always clash with someone's personal agenda. This ensures an early demise for any concept that has to work its way up the organization for final approval.

Boy, was she right. Over the years I've learned that brilliant thinking never wins the day on its own merits. If you don't have the right people in the room, effective positioning becomes a long shot at best.

Old Cash Cows

The first type of obstacle a new positioning idea will often encounter is that of an old cash cow. New positioning ideas tend to be built on new opportunities, which can sometimes challenge old businesses. The result is a reluctance to foster the new ideas. Peter Drucker calls this "slaughtering tomorrow's opportunity on the altar of yesterday."

In that meeting at a large computer manufacturer, I was encouraging them to position their new line of workstations as PMs or Personal Mainframes. This obviously would have upset the head of the mainframe business, a business that was still throwing off big profits. At the other end of the spectrum, the head of the personal computer business probably would have complained as well.

Only the CEO could have made this decision to pursue a concept that potentially could have attacked his biggest cash cow. And since he wasn't in the room, he never had a chance to consider a strategy which, today, looks pretty good, when you consider the industry trend toward desktop machines.

The most successful companies are quite good at attacking their cash cows. Gillette is a prime example. First they slaughtered their single-edge and stainless blades with the highly successful twin-bladed razor (Trac II). Then they attacked that idea with an adjustable twin-bladed razor (Atra). Then came the shock-absorbing razor (Sensor). And now they've come up with a sensor with fins. It's called Sensor Excel. If they come up with a better idea, they'll use it against themselves.

Old Bad Decisions

Another problem with not having the right people in the room is the ghost of old bad decisions.

New strategies often clash with prior decisions. In my 25 years of strategic work, no one has ever said to me, "We're glad you've arrived. We've been doing nothing while we've been waiting for you to get here."

Obviously they've been doing a lot, some of which wasn't working very well. (People don't call you when things are good.)

Unfortunately, no one in a large corporation wants to admit to making a bad decision. Especially a bad *big* decision. This is particularly true in an organization that isn't very good at tolerating failure. As a result, it goes against almost all middle-level managers' instincts to embrace any new idea that could cause them embarrassment about their old decisions.

Where Were You When I Needed You?

I'll never forget sitting in the office of an office products company and laying out a positioning strategy that essentially challenged their soon-to-be-announced effort to try to sell a new generation of computer systems. At the end of the session, a very senior executive looked me in the eye and said: "Where were you when I needed you two years ago?" (Two years ago this bad decision was sent to the Board of Directors for initial approval.)

Even though this executive now realized it was the wrong decision, he was saying to me that he couldn't admit to a mistake of that magnitude. Understandable from his point of view, but tragic from the company's point of view. Especially when you consider that a competitor took the same strategy and built a multibillion-dollar business around it.

Only the CEO was in a position to change the plans, and he wasn't in the room.

"I'm in Charge Here"

Another problem you may encounter is the "corporate ego" of your immediate superiors or your advertising agency. They may have a problem with an outsider doing their job. "After all," they'll say to themselves, "*I'm* in charge. If I accept someone else's thinking, my superiors will think less of me."

This can be a very difficult situation. I've discovered that, rather than dismiss an "outside" recommendation out-of-hand, this type of person invariably adds his or her own thinking to the situation. Makes his or her contribution, so to speak. What results is a modified strategy that isn't really the same. It's like changing a cake's recipe. It may look the same, but it sure doesn't taste like the same cake. (Advertising agencies are especially good at this kind of modification.)

The higher you are presenting in an organization, the less likely you are to come across these kinds of ego problems.

Advice for the Cautious

If, for some reason, getting the right people in the room isn't feasible, you'll have to find a way to get the CEO involved in the process. Without that involvement, your strategy will never be implemented properly. So the trick is to carefully construct a case that your superiors can be comfortable with, as they carry it upward to the CEO.

For example, you might include what I call "the world has changed" section at the beginning of your presentation. This automatically communicates the idea that when the earlier decisions were taken (rightly or wrongly), they appeared correct at that time.

The purpose of this kind of language is to soothe egos by masking the earlier mistake. Also, the notion of a changing world makes it sound more like a decision the CEO should take a look at.

But this may not be enough.

Use an Analogy

Rather than just toss that terrifying-looking decision onto the table, you might want to consider prefacing it with an analogous case study drawn from somewhere in corporate history.

That way, you're saying "XYZ Company tried something similar, and bad things happened to them." Don't forget to add, "Of course, it may not happen to us."

Believe me, when confronted with someone else's mistakes, people get a lot more objective. The person you're presenting to will say to himself, "With my luck, that *will* happen to us. I'd better show this to the boss."

Implement Slowly

Finally, implement any difficult positioning strategy slowly, especially if it's of the "repositioning" kind.

People need time to adjust to change. By making changes slowly, you reduce the anxiety that comes with a dramatic shift of strategy.

As someone once said: "Most people can survive the old way. Most people can survive the new way. It's the *transition* that'll kill you."

Many years ago, Al Ries and I advised Burger King to hang "Kiddieland" on McDonald's and reposition Burger King as the place for grown-ups and grown-up kids. This would mean sacrificing a part of the market to McDonald's, not to mention eliminating swing sets from their franchisees' facilities.

This represented a major shift in strategy, and it created instant anxiety. The only way to sell this idea was on a "test it and roll it out slowly" basis. Unfortunately, "anxiety" won out over "slowly," and an opportunity was missed.

This all points to the inescapable fact that "positioning" is serious stuff. It sets the direction for a company's business strategy. And when serious decisions are being made, top management must be in the room.

Business is a battle of ideas that play out in the mind of the prospect. (My position versus your position.)

If you don't have a simple, differentiating idea to drive your company or brand, you'd better have a great price.

INDEX

ABOUT THE AUTHORS

JACK TROUT revisits the concept he introduced in 1969 in this engrossing new book. The acclaimed coauthor of five best-selling books, he is president of Trout & Partners Ltd., a Greenwich, Connecticut, marketing strategy firm that has consulted for leading corporations such as AT&T, Merck, IBM, Southwest Airlines, and Warner-Lambert.

STEVE RIVKIN worked with Jack Trout for 15 years, then founded his own communications consulting firm in Midland Park, New Jersey. Rivkin & Associates Inc. has worked for clients such as Chase Manhattan Bank, Monsanto, Pfizer's Howmedica Inc., and Tiffany & Co.

"Positioning" in the World of Business

"A firm in a highly attractive industry may still not earn satisfactory profits if it has chosen a poor competitive **positioning.**"

MICHAEL E. PORTER
The Competitive Advantage of Nations

"The key to any marketing plan is **positioning.**"

RON ZARRELLA
VICE PRESIDENT, GENERAL MOTORS
Brandweek

"IKEA will review its **positioning** and what the company will stand for in the future.**"**

Svenska Dagbladet (Sweden)

"The company is an upstart preparing for a showdown with almighty Microsoft, and is **positioning** itself as the anti-Gates.**"**

Fortune

"The global marketing imperative: **Positioning** your company for the new world of business.**"**

Chicago Tribune

"The shift of focus from hardware to software and the success of companies like Microsoft have undermined IBM's **positioning** as the leading computer company.**"**

Computer World Sweden

"Positioning is the spearhead in strategic thinking.**"**

NieuwsTribune (Holland)

"The basic **positioning** for Nickelodeon came out of a series of research meetings in 1984.**"**

Los Angeles Times

"Success in Luxembourg results of clear **positioning.**"

DEUTSCHE GIROZENTRALE ADVERTISEMENT
Financial Times, London